#LUNCHBOXCHRONICLES:

Raising a Conscious Black Boy in America

TAI HALL

Focused Futures

Published by Focused Futures Publishing

Contact:

P.O. Box 29686
Baltimore, MD 21216

TheLunchBoxChronicles.com
connect@thelunchboxchronicles.com

Publishing Coordination by Brown & Duncan Brand. BandDBrand.com
ISBN: 978-0-9992023-4-0

Printed in the United States of America

DEDICATED TO THE UNITS

Thanks for the best sermon I could ever hear: the word "no."
I am forever grateful to you for trusting me to stand on my own.

CONTENTS

INICIO

Heroes to Hashtags

I started writing *Lunch Box Chronicles* a few years ago as a means of venting. Using Facebook as a platform, I gave myself a soapbox. Before then? I was subjected to laughs and giggles from my parents about my parenting woes. They proved to be of little help, by the way. It dawned on me at the beginning of my son's second-grade school year that he was pretty forgetful. By the sixth week of school, he had lost, well misplaced, (in his terms) three coats, four hats, and two lunch boxes. I hit the ceiling. Frustrated, I called my heroes... my parents. They always made everything better from bike accidents to broken hearts; from stupid boys to my "can I borrow $50?" requests. But not this time. Ohhhh heroes have limits.

I started fussing to my mom, who I actually never called mom. She was either "Ma" or "Lady." I told her everything, seeking some help or advice. Instead? I got giggles.

"That's what you get 'lil girl! I've been waiting for this day. You lost EVERYTHING when you were his age. Here I am working hard to take care of you, send you out the house looking nice... and you could care less. Stockings full of holes, skirt on backwards, penny loafers scraped up. 'Tai, where's your hat?'

'Tai, where's your scarf?'

'Tai… what happened to your lunch box?!'

Your answer was always the same:

'I don't know what happened mommy.' I even sent you out of here one day dressed to the nines with the cutest little diamond earrings on. Nothing for you to do except to come home with only one stud in your ear. And as always, your answer was: 'Uhhhmmm I don't know mommy, but I love you.' So little girl, I don't feel sorry for you."

I was thinking to myself… *Who puts 1 carat diamonds on a seven-year old ANYWAYS?!*

But, my siblings and I learned quickly, no matter how old we were, not to sass my mom. We were either hung up on or threatened that she would jump through the phone and slap the taste out of our mouths for being disrespectful. While that may be impossible for the average mom, my momma has never been average. She continued carrying on about how I deserved everything her grandson was putting me through, and she thanked God that He let her live long enough to see it all.

(smh).

Once my dad looked down at the caller ID and saw who had called he couldn't wait to chime in. At that point, I knew I wasn't going to get any help from the units. They continued to swap stories about everything I had lost over my childhood—ranging from four retainers after my braces were removed, countless house keys, cell phones, clothes, books, pens... By the time I managed to get off of the phone with them, not only did I not have a solution of what to do with my forgetful son, but my parents had given me a verbal invoice in the neighborhood of $17,000, a ballpark estimate of all the things I had lost and they had replaced until I graduated high school.

I wasn't about to continue this parenting thing operating as a living definition of insanity—replacing items only for my son to lose them again. So, in spirit of any Generation X parent, where did I turn for refuge, resources, and solutions? Where all the millennials go for truth and knowledge—Facebook of course.

I started posting my and 'convos' with The Kid, (he's always been "The Kid" and my brother has always been "The Boy." My dad? He was Eric,) and I asked other moms how they effectively handled their forgetful children. While I received some great answers from other moms who had mastered this parenting thing, they quickly informed me of how entertaining our stories were. Someone sent me a Facebook message and said, "Hey, you should name your posts with a hashtag called "#LunchBoxChronicles."

People looked forward to our madness. That's what my household has always been: organized dysfunction, or in layman's terms, madness. The "#LunchBoxChronicles" soon turned into God-guided life experiences about raising a young black boy in today's society. These lessons are somewhat timeless and seemed repetitive of every decade. Although I've never studied in an African American studies textbook, nothing seems to change. We rally, we protest, we march, and the resulting racism persists just a tad bit more covert each time. And while I acknowledge there is only so much I can do to protect my son from the world, the best source of armor I can equip him with is that of life experiences and raw knowledge.

I had The Kid when I was extremely young. I was a kid myself. A kid raising a kid, I didn't know what I was doing. To be honest, to this day, I still don't. Through trial and error, each day that I don't lose him, forget to feed him, or leave him somewhere unintentionally random is a victory for me (and all young moms everywhere).

I've been figuring it out. Our lives seemed to unfold slowly as a beautiful haphazard mess of struggle and uncomfortable growth. The reality of this journey of parenthood unveiled racism within a post-civil and spiritual war, disrupting my little one's innocence and replacing it with a commanding consciousness of color and socioeconomic disparity.

As life wind-stormed with us, locked and loaded on this fast-paced roller-coaster, strapped in for the long haul—hands thrown up and eyes closed, we spiraled out of control experiencing police brutality, covert prejudice, discrimination, a disability label, and I often found myself wondering, "How am I to raise my son among this madness?! Do I tell him that he can successfully grow up to be anything he wants to be in this world except **black**?"

The roller coaster continued; hell, it sped up as life always does. And we corralled on figuring out the plot twists and dodging bullets as they came. One school-bound "How was your day kiddo?" conversation, one unpredictable adventure across the fifty states, and one lost lunch box at a time.

#LUNCHBOXCHRONICLES

Capítulo Uno
#PrinceGeorgesCounty
{Antes}

March 20, 2014

Yo...Anyone ever stop..and stare at their kid...Like Holy Crap someone gave me a kid?! And you start to process that you're in charge of another human? This epiphany of responsibility washes over you: I...have...a..kid. I'm not sure that's ever going to fully sink in lol no matter how old he gets.

September 16, 2014 - Largo, MD

About to spend the morning in the zoo that is to be Kingsford Elementary with a bunch of overzealous parents & hyped 2nd graders. Wish me luck!

This was our second school so far since starting the great educational adventure known as elementary school. His first was a private school associated with the church we had been attending for a few months since moving back to Prince Georges County, Maryland. The school was new and extended from Pre-K to high school. It was the school's second year in operation and the administration was looking for ways to grow their attendance numbers and performance scores. Somehow, a teacher received an earful about how smart my son was as a result of him attending the children's ministry during Sunday service. Not too long after, we were approached by the school treasurer asking if I would consider enrolling him in their private school program for the upcoming academic year at a fifty percent discounted rate.

I mulled it over and decided to give it a whirl. He was there for no longer than three weeks before the school principal approached me in the parking lot. She knew what my son looked like before school started; we attended all of the orientation meetings, all of the meet and greets, and each of the back-to-school nights. Yet there we were three weeks into the semester and this robustly rotund lady ran over to me in the parking lot one brisk morning in dire need to have a conversation.

My coffee hadn't kicked in and my estrogen was low; she definitely picked the wrong day to rap but *let's go,* I thought.

She proceeded to inform me that while they loved having my son as a part of their school family, they had a "no hair policy."

"A no hair policy," I repeated confused, because as I had mentioned, they *knew what my son looked like.* My son, Kordelle, was a bubbly first grader who had been skipped to the second grade, (to be later put back into his age appropriate grade) and he lived a care-free life, unaware of the spiritual and worldly attacks going on around him.

Being raised by a free-spirit, care-free momma, he also never had a haircut. Not for religious purposes, just because, well, we didn't want one. He had hair that, when freshly braided or blown out, came to the top of his pants. He was six going on seven and had no intentions to cut his hair anytime soon. This was fine with me as it saved me the hassle and expense of haircuts.

I stared at the overbearing woman for a second posturing myself before fully responding, and then I said aloud what I had been thinking in my head, "But you knew what my son looked like before we came here… did you think we were going to change for you? All of the men in my family have long hair…except for Eric…he's bald and he blames me, but that's another story. I'm sorry, but my son's hair is his choice and that's not negotiable."

The principal pursed her lips and then informed me, "Well he may finish out the school year, but he will not be able to return for any subsequent years until you cut his hair. I already have parents furious with me because their sons had to receive haircuts to attend this school, but see your boy running around with a head full of hair."

My son interjected and said, "Yea mommy, one lady stopped and asked me if I was a girl! I told her nope I have a penis."

Pause. "You have adults approaching my child?! Why are you more concerned with his appearance than his protection?! At no time should any adult be placing their hands on my son pulling him aside to have any types of conversations without a teacher or professional figure being present," I quipped back. "Furthermore, why are you more concerned with what is on my son's head than what's in it?!"

The principal told me that my headstrongness would get in the way of my son's educational success, boisterously noting the struggle of our young black men in the professional world, being slighted for their appearances. She, as well as the other educators, had taken a stance to uphold the "no hair policy" to give the boys a fighting chance within the professional world in their futures. I was also informed that maybe not at this moment, but sometime in the future, I needed to give serious consideration to my desire to maintain my son's appearance.

I paused, took a deep breath, and informed her that her establishment was not a part of the solution, but they were all a part of the problem. "You ma'am see nothing wrong with bowing down to the powers that may be in this world, cowering yourself, changing your looks, perming your coils, pressing your naps, and cutting your locs to appease the masses.

Instead of encouraging our boys to soar above the obstacles placed against them within the societal constructs—to not simply settle for being labeled "good" whilst allowing people to control their looks and value, you would rather discourage them from being who they really are. You aren't pushing them to be great. No ma'am, YOU encourage them to conform.

Don't let my tattoos or my piercings fool you. I *know* who I am, where I come from, and the stamp my family will make on society no matter *what* we look like. I don't need to wait to address your concerns of my desire to maintain my son's hair: *YOU* are his first educators. But *I* am his first teacher. And altering how he looks to placate to you or anyone else will *NEVER* be a lesson that he will learn. Please check your cowardice at the door next time you step to a woman who knows her worth."

Her eyes grew as big as saucers, and before she could respond, I placed my flattened palm in front of her face and told her to save it. "We need not converse any longer. We good." I marched in the church, withdrew my son that morning, and then enrolled him in our local public elementary school by the close of business that day.

As we were sitting in the office of his new school, he asked me why we were transferring. He liked the other school. I told him that I would never allow someone to treat him any differently because of how he looks. He said, "Ok."

October 13, 2014
So in love with being a mom.

December 3, 2014 6:13PM - Watkins Park, MD
SO excited to pick my son up from his aftercare. Haven't seen that guy since this morning I miss him! In love w/ my mini me.

I need to pause here. This day for some reason, I was extra excited to pick up The Kid. For no reason, absolutely no reason at all. It wasn't a holiday or any event going on. We weren't headed anywhere special. I wasn't hormonal, on my period, feeling extra lovey-dovey with a dash of rage lingering on the tip of my tongue, nope. I was just dumb happy to go pick up my mini on a regular random day of the week. But as soon as I got to him, all that dissipated.

December 3, 2014 6:34PM
THIS DUDE GOT ME FEELING EMOTIONALLY BIPOLAR! I JUST put up a post about how in love I am... (Deep breath) this kid has lost 3 lunch bags, 2 engraved rings, & 4 hats since Aug. I SPECIFICALLY said this morning, "do NOT come into this house without a lunch bag today or I'm going to spank you!"...WHY IS HE LUNCHBAGLESS?! Are my threats a joke?! But I don't want to spank him why is he making me do this?! He coulda copped somebody else's lunch bag and I would've dealt. But he is empty handed?! He was bold enough to have the audacity to be that careless to have NO lunch box?! Why WHY would he test my parental skills?! And now I HAVE to spank him bc I promised him one...But I just knew he would come home with it...Smh #singleparentproblems

I had actually forgotten that I told him I would spank him if he lost his lunch box again. Ole Honest Abe reminded me, "Mommy does that mean I get a spanking like you said this morning?" My mental process, "Dudeeeeee…why you 'gotta word it like that? That means I most definitely HAVE TO spank you now!" I couldn't be a pushover parent—the one who promised to spank their kid if he lost his lunch box again when he was seven, but let him slide. Nope, I had to do the inevitable to stand my ground. If not, that once innocent seven-year-old would grow to be seven-teen, full blown out of control, with no respect for any adult—ESPE-CIALLY not the single mom who busted her butt to raise him while working several odd-end jobs. My child would not grow up a displaced, pot-smoking hippie who has communication issues, lacks self-control, steals, gets sent to jail, locked up and for me to have to visit him on evenings and weekends, because he got a racist cop and an unfair trial,

"JUDGE IT WAS HIS FIRST OFFENSE! HE DIDN'T MEAN IT!" NO! Not my kid. I HAD to spank him! If I didn't hold true to my word, this would develop a premise in his mind that I made empty promises and threats.

He low-key sniffled during the entire car ride home. We walked to his room; I found one of his belts, told him to pull down his pants, pulled my hand back and…

All I heard in my head was my father's voice, "This is going to hurt me way more than it's going to hurt you." Back then when I was a kid, I thought that was the stupidest saying ever. How could it possibly hurt him when HE HAD THE BELT?! *My butt is getting lashed sir, not yours!*

Now I knew. I felt awful after spanking him. He didn't even cry for real. Nope. He did one of those 'my soul is dying' cries. The one where his mouth opens up, he takes a deep breath in, but nothing, not even the breath of God, could be heard coming out of him for like five seconds. And then he whimpered from sucking his lower lip back in real fast three or four times. Yep, he did that. He sat down on the bed, and tears fell down his rosy cheeks as he pulled his pants up but still never actually made any real noises.

I felt so bad. So bad that we baked cookies and munched in silence as we watched *Black-ish*. I think I cried that night. Worst night ever…'til the day I found out he had a girlfriend, and I was no longer the only lady in his life. Then THAT became the worst night ever.

December 4, 2014 6:29PM
If he knows what's good for him… He better NOT be lunchboxless today…

Spoiler alert!..

HE HAD A LUNCH BOX THAT DAY! I was sooooo happy that I didn't have to spank him. I know "they" say, "Spare the rod and spoil the child," but you know… maybe spoiled kids aren't totally that bad? I turned out decent and I'm spoiled rotten (Just don't ask my boyfriend his opinion on the matter. Let's just take my word for it).

I digress (insert defeated shrug HERE). I was just so elated that I took The Kid to his favorite restaurant when I picked him up: The Blue Dolphin in Crofton, Maryland. We dined and giggled and laughed, then headed home where I unloaded the car and unpacked his book bag.

December 4, 2014 6:42PM
HE HAS A LUNCHBOX!…Except, it isn't his smdh. It's not even the same color. He looked at me & said, "You told me don't come home without a lunchbox. You didn't say it had to be mine." WTF…#iQuit

December 8, 2014

Mommy: how was your day baby?

Kordelle: it was great! I brought a lunch bag home & everything!

Mommy: but Kordelle, I gave you money to buy school lunch...I didn't send you to school with a lunch bag.

Kordelle: I know. But you told me last week I better not come home without a lunchbox...Does that not apply anymore?

...crickets...crickets....

I've traumatized my kid. Smh. Wait... pause...Whose lunchbox is he stealing and bringing home though?! #iGiveUp!

I was rushing that morning, handed the kid some money for lunch, and we jetted out of the door. So of course, I was caught off guard when I picked him up that evening and he had a lunch box. I was completely confused because I hadn't sent him out of the house with a lunch box...He took that "You better not be lunch box-less" thing literal! Part of me wanted to die laughing at the smartass I was raising. The other half was beyond concerned at who's lunch box he had? (Insert super surprised emoji face HERE.)

December 9, 2014

#LunchBoxChronicles

As I unpack his lunchbox and fuss about random inequalities in life, Kordelle interjects: "Mom...Calm down. If every pork chop was perfect, we wouldn't have hotdogs. It's going to be ok."

...crickets...crickets...

WTF does that mean?! I'm raising Yoda.

December 17, 2014
#LunchBoxChronicles
Mommy: SO! Kid! What're you bringing home today?
Kordelle: my lunchbox, some stuff & some more stuff
Mommy: stuff? So everything else is irrelevant huh? Lol
Kordelle: (ignores question) Mom why can't I have a baby brother?
...crickets...crickets...

Mommy: Bc I'm not married
Kordelle: do you at least have a boyfriend?
Mommy: nooo...nahhh...I'muhhh... Actually going in the opposite direction there buddy
Kordelle: soooo... You uuuuhhh...Have... Aaaaa Girl...Friend?
Mommy: WTH kid no!
Kordelle: I'm just saying! Hear me out! I was watching the news & that thing is legal in MD now and it would double my chances of getting a baby brother. You should keep your options open.

My son tried to convince me to be a lesbian! Shout out to rainbow beauties, but that just has never been my cup of tea. While my son was in love with CNN and NBC, and Rachel Maddow, I think he was a bit too young to understand the full concept of how babies are made. And I was in no mood to inform him that 1 + 1 does not always equal two. The birds and the bees were going to have to wait. At least until I'd had a cup of coffee [with a shot of Jack].

December 18, 2014 - Mitchellville, MD

The moment you discover your superheroes aren't that heroic... They're simply flawed humans that you once looked up to that only tried their best smh...#sigh

I just aim to be better than. BETTER THAN WHAT?

My dad and I got into the worst fight ever one morning at 6 a.m. Screaming and yelling and crying. Lots of crying. I guess me moving back home to hit the restart button on life took a toll on everyone, especially my dad. My parents have always loved me, but we didn't always see eye-to-eye. I have always loved my parents, to the moon and back. They were my biggest supporters, whether I was spot on or dead-ass wrong. Mannnn...the long-drawn-out conversations that I would have with my dad for hours until 4 a.m. were priceless and so was the shoulder my mom provided anytime a guy broke my heart. They fought my battles and showed me how to win wars. They fixed boo-boos, showed me how to tie my shoes, taught me how to fight, how to cook, how to get rid of hangovers—my parents were my rocks. There wasn't a thing they couldn't fix... or so I thought. But that cold mean morning? My world came crashing down when reality hit me in the face like a bag of soggy socks.

What do you do, when the ones who once only helped are now the ones who hurt you?

All I wanted to do was cry when I realized my heroes—the very people who would put me back together again when life kicked my ass—were basic, normal humans just like you and I. Flawed, imperfect, don't-have-all-the-answers humans. "What do you mean you messed up and you're sorry? You're a parent, MY parent...you...you make mistakes?"

I just couldn't wrap my mind around this concept. What do you do when your heroes aren't that heroic? It was like the day I found out wrestling wasn't real, what scrapple was made of, that there is no Saint Nick. I sat and cried for hours driving home after feeling so hurt by the realization. My light bulb moment caused by the horrible explosive argument I had with my dad before the sun rose is forever ingrained in my mind and I immediately became scared. Whether I had a kid or not, I wasn't a child anymore. And my heroes? They could no longer fight my battles for me. I… I had to grow up. #neverfeltsoalone

Did some serious soul searching and after several days of healing, I moved out of my parents' home for the last time. Healing takes time and everyone grieves differently. And while it sounds ideal to snap your fingers and mosey through the grieving process quickly, I got stuck on that anger part. I was angry at my parents for being flawed. I was angry for having to grow up. I was angry at…sigh, I was angry and disappointed in myself.

It took me almost two years to fix what was broken during that last argument with my dad. I prayed a lot. I cried even more. Every time I drove past the main road where my parents lived, my eyes would well up, knowing that my ego mixed with pain wouldn't let me make the right turn into their neighborhood. So I would just continue driving straight. I searched through the volcano of emotions for enough strength to be my son's hero. However, unlike my parents, I allowed myself room to be human. You see, I never EVER saw my parents argue. I never saw them go through anything, never saw them *grow* through anything. I didn't learn conflict resolution until I was twenty-nine years old.

While my parents may have seen their lack of transparency involving conflicts as a way to protect me, it wound up crippling me. I had no idea that they were flawed, besides, they were HEROES! I mean after the fact, yea Eric and I talked about how he tried to do his best by me, but he made mistakes along the way. Mistakes? But you were—are a hero, was all I could think. When did heroes ever mess up? You ever see Superman drop anyone out of the sky while carrying them to safety? Nope, sure didn't. The mom from The Incredibles fought bad guys and was home in time to have dinner ready by 6 p.m. AND maintained perfect hair while doing so. Okay, maybe I watched way too much television and read too many comics as a kid, but my skewed realism paralleled reality my entire life. My parent superheroes had always been just as strong, just as unstoppable, and just as perfect as all the make belief superheroes on television.

Who knew raising your kid "right" could end so wrong? Thus, while protecting my son from life's disrespectful rawness and a false sense of perfectionism, I occasionally lean over to him, look him in his eyes, and say, "You do know I have no idea what I am doing right?" He keels over in laughter, reaches up to give me a kiss, and says, "Mom you're doing alright by me."

At the moment, that's all I can ask for.

#LUNCHBOXCHRONICLES

CAPÍTULO DOS

#ComfortZonesAreOverrated

{Una flor no importa...}

December 23, 2014- Hyattsville, MD

#LunchBoxChronicles

Mommy: Kordelle...Why is the snack cabinet empty?! Where are all of my canned foods & your lunch snacks?

Kordelle: oh...I donated them

Mommy: WTF...All of them?! WHY?!!!!!! When did you even take all this stuff & I didn't see it...How...Kordelle WTF?!

Kordelle: I asked you could I help out the less fortunate you said "yes"! Remember the day you made me take all the lunchboxes back that weren't mine?

Pause.

Long pregnant pause.

Ok. THIS DUDE (insert face to palm emoji HERE) smh. Around this time, I was finishing up graduate school. I was pursuing a master's degree in healthcare, and my studies were legit kicking my butt. Quite often, I would fall asleep on the couch and conveniently wake up ten minutes past the time that we needed to have left the house.

I hadn't perfected this parenting thing quite yet, thus packing lunches the day before seemed too much like right. I had been rushing to get us out of the door and him to school on time. I would literally throw him into a clean uniform. Then, I'd grab the car keys, his book bag, and my driver's license (in case a cop decided to flex while I was flying up the road).

I would do school "drive-by" drop offs, give him lunch money, and pause to blow him a kiss before pulling off. No matter how late or behind we were, the mini loved "love" as much as I and would blow me a kiss every day before turning to go into the building. He screamed at the top of his lungs one day chasing behind my car, "MOM WAITTTTTTTTTT!" I slammed on brakes thinking that I perhaps was about to hit a gang of puppies by the sound of his wail. All he wanted was to blow me a kiss goodbye.

I was working extra-long hours as I was saving to buy our first house. Kordelle had an aunt who would help us out on my super late days. She had a key to my place; would pick him up, bring him to our apartment, unpack his bag, and heat up whatever grub I had fixed for dinner earlier that morning before jetting up the highway to work. All of this to say: I didn't check his book bag for his lunch box for about a week or so. My life eventually slowed down after about a week, and our household chaos went back to a normal, tolerable level.

I opened the cabinet where I kept our lunch boxes to pack his lunch for the day and saw about five bags in there that I hadn't bought. After asking the kid where they had come from, he reminded me that I told him he couldn't come in the house without a lunch box.

Pause.

Long pregnant pause.

He had been BUYING school lunch for about a week. WHERE WAS HE GETTING THESE LUNCH BOXES FROM?!

Furious at his need to be literal, I demanded that he return all of the rogue lunch boxes. He finished getting dressed as I packed our lunches, came into the kitchen, and asked if he could donate some food to the homeless. He explained that his school was having a holiday food drive, and he wanted to help the less fortunate. I was so proud of my mini me that I told him of course.

I left him in the kitchen to pick out which cans he wanted to donate and went to my room to get dressed. I always require my son to load bags, such as groceries or travel suitcases into and out of the truck. I opt to raise a chivalrous child who embodies qualities that I see lacking in the men I date (Dear his future wife: You're welcome).

He packed the car, I finished getting dressed, and up the road we went. I dropped him off at school; he grabbed all of his items from the back seat with all of the "borrowed" lunch boxes in tow. I blew him a kiss. Ahhhh our "thing," no matter who was around, he blew me a kiss. I drove off into the sunrise; geez I love that Kid! [Keep in mind, if you pick up on where this is going before I break it down any further to all of you judgmental perfect parents out there: I was… am, a stressed, single-parent-college-kid lacking my own observational skills—with a personal plight of ADHD.]

I picked him up that afternoon, and he had HIS lunch box and only HIS lunch box! I smothered him in kisses, and we drove home.

The next morning, I reach into the cupboard to pack his lunch and discovered the cupboard was empty. I immediately went off the deep end (as usual in typical Tai fashion) screaming, "OMG we've been robbed! Someone robbed me! They took all my food. ALL MY FOOD! Wait… they stole my food, but not my 55" LED TV? What my TV not good enough for them? Who steals food, but not the television?!" We lived in the hood. A decent hood. But "hood" nonetheless. First floor apartment with no bars on the window and a less-than-stellar front door. The apartment building housed four units, so I suspected it was someone in the building being as though none of the windows were broken. (Side note: *Scandal* tainted normal life for me after Season 2).

It was nothing for Kordelle to come out to check on me and my commotion. He calmly explained that we hadn't been robbed, but he had packed up all of the dry food to give to the less fortunate, in the rogue lunch boxes he had to return. He was quite proud of himself for killing two birds with one stone. I lost it, "GOT DAMMIT KORDELLE. WE AREEEEEEEEE THE LESS FORTUNATE!"

Earlier this particular year, my mini came home overly excited from school. Bubbly, he blurted out, "Mommy did you know that there are fifty states?!" He exclaimed with the biggest, brightest eyes as if HE was the one who had discovered all of them (insert super wide eyes HERE). I laughed and said, "Nooooo! Really? Get outa here!" Kordelle then stated with complete conviction, "And we are going to see all fifty!" The look on my face must have said it all. His little smile dropped, "Right mommy?" I looked at the kid and tried to explain the value of a dollar all in that moment when I told him, "Baby that sounds mighty expensive. You know mommy is saving for a house right?"

He bolted to his room as I continued to sift through his lunch box and unpack his bag without a response. Kordelle came back with a tattered plastic wallet I had given him a few years back and pulled out two crumpled dollars. He handed them to me proudly and said, "Here mommy. I can help. Will THIS get us to the fifty states?"

I took the money from my son and said, "It's a start baby." My heroes always encouraged me no matter how crazy or outlandish my dreams were. I was to do the same for him. I also started to devise a plan to teach the kid about money along the way, because between his constant forgetfulness and our new travel ventures, we would BOTH have to start budgeting, honestly, acknowledging the differences between a 'want' and a 'need'.

Some people gamble, some people drink. Our vice? We travel now. I had initially suggested that instead of travelling that we find photos of different states and write research papers. He wasn't having any of that. Kordelle harped about it for so many weeks in a row that I finally gave in, and we took a road trip to Delaware for the weekend. Sigh, fifty states—here we come! I didn't forego on those research papers though. Post-toddler or not, he owed me. I told him as a trade-off for paying, driving, tour guiding, he owed me a research paper for every state we visited. And thus, our adventures began. I should have added a stipulation for him to keep up with his lunch box along with the research papers.

December 31, 2014 2:12PM (at the Sixth Floor Museum: JFK Dealey Plaza exhibit)- Dallas, TX

Mommy: Kordelle...I need you to tell the lady that you're 5yrs old
Kordelle: but...why? I'm not 5, I'm almost 8
Mommy: because it will save me $25
Kordelle: so...You want me to lie? But you told me lying is wrong
Mommy: when it can save mommy money it's not AS wrong
Kordelle: ok. Pay me $20...
Mommy: WHAT?!...TF?!
Kordelle: You still save money!
Mommy: I will leave you in this great state of Texas, you cannot extort me TF is wrong with you??!!!
Kordelle: soooo...You want me to say 5 or 8?

     We had made our way to the south. This specific trip was unintentionally ironic in that we visited Arkansas (where President Clinton was from), Texas (where the Bush's were from), and Chicago (Obama's hometown). None of this is relevant to the story, but the coincidence of it all made me smile.

December 31, 2014 11:13PM- Houston, TX

Mommy: man its late. WELP...Guess we gotta head back to the hotel & go to sleep

Kordelle: why? I'm not sleepy it's so early!
Mommy: everything closed kid
Kordelle: nope! The bar is still open! We can chill there.

To note, the bar was connected to an indoor theme park equipped with rides, games, bumper cars; it even had a pretty nice "divey" type of food joint in the middle. Just a big ole setup to steal our money. If they don't know how to do anything else right in Texas, they know how to make money.

January 2, 2015- Austin, TX

Smh...When being a mom gets real...
I HATE those moms whose hair is laid, nails done, outfit on fleek... & their child looks a hot mess. I'm standing next to Kordelle at baggage check-in...Noticed how ashy his lips were and FREAKED!
Mommy: you look like whodunnitandwhatfor! You look like your mother doesn't love you! What is going on with the extra layer of crust growing on your lips?! Stay still and let me put chap stick on you!
Kordelle: NOOOoooo mom we're in public! You're going to embarrass me!
Mommy: YOUVE ALREADY BEEN DOING THAT APPARENTLY ALL MORNING, stay still!
Kordelle: no ma you go overboard with the chap stick!
Mommy: (attacks, tackles, & applies chap stick) THERE all better!

In the middle of 'de-ashyfying' my kid and his attempts to struggle free, he knocked over his bag... That then knocks over EVERY. OTHER. BAG—Domino-style—that was waiting to be loaded onto the conveyor belt (for about three different flights).I looked up to a slew of angry employees, because I had definitely just 'confuddled' their work loads.

When I noticed their lips were ashy too.
Mommy: "aye look bruh...Keep looking at me like that & ALL yall can get this chap stick werk too!!!"
...at least my kid aint ashy lipped chappy no more
#ArkansasBound

As we traipsed through Arkansas, I made sure to take him to the museums. He learned about HIV and AIDs from Ryan White, who became a national poster child for HIV/AIDS in the United States after failing to be re-admitted to school following an AIDS diagnosis. We also learned about the life of Anne Frank and the struggles of Ruby Bridges. I took him to Central High, where he learned about the Little Rock Nine; together we listened to the horror stories and traced the lives of the teens throughout the country's first years of school integration.

He saw the "white only" signs and water fountains. We discussed how his white friends in school NOW came at a cost. I took him to see the movie *Selma* when it was first released, while we happened to still be in the south. We discussed the socioeconomic gap that has been created amongst cultures and ethnicities due to the residual effects of discrimination.

Nothing compares to explaining racism and prejudices due to the color of one's skin as much as seeing it play out in the present day. As we drove through Arkansas, even WITH a GPS, I got lost. We had gotten quite a ways away from the touristy areas on the beaten paths we had been traveling. As I drove through the poverty-ridden streets of Little Rock, I told my son to put down his Gameboy and *look*. He closed his Nintendo DS and looked out the window. I asked him to tell me what he saw. I wanted to make sure that what he was witnessing with his untainted mind was actually registering. He described trees and buildings.

I prompted him, "What else do you see?" He pointed out that the buildings, the houses, were in poor shape. He noted that there was not any grass.

"What else do you see?" The sidewalks were cracked and the kids were running around with holes in their shoes. Their coats were open and their clothes were dirty. This was all from the mouth of a now awakened child.

I have traveled the world and back again, and being in the streets of Arkansas reminded me of neighborhoods in developing nations not the land of "the free." I remember checking into our hotel and trying to schedule a cab to take us downtown (before I got fed-up and rented a car). The vernacular of the front desk personnel, his undereducated speech, the way he referred to his boss as 'the man' all disgusted me. I wanted to pull him close and whisper in his ear with a deep southern drawl, "You do know that we's free now right?"

When I went back and read my son's research paper on Arkansas, he noted how blessed he felt to have a video game system, shoes without holes, and grass. While us adults squander over what labels are on our backs, a child is happy to have grass. Let that sink in. #wewillnotcomplain

January 3, 2015 - Little Rock, AR

Fell down stairs. Dropped keys in marsh (go read the bridge story). Keys are electronic and were sitting in a shallow marsh... I love crackheads.

They will forever hold a place in my heart. And they maintain a certain importance in American Society. Sho'l did pay a crackhead $5 to go get my keys. #crackheadsforpresident

The bridge story: I tell Kordelle, "Be careful walking down these stairs" as we're leaving the bridge...

I slip.

Fall.

Hands go flailing in the air and electronic car keys to the rental car go flying over the 'effin bridge and land in a marsh. A wet. Watery. Marsh. Kordelle started dying laughing and said, "Mommy you should be careful walking down these stairs!" A marsh. A mutha effin marsh. I wasn't going in the marsh. Lies. I had to go in it... How else was I going to get the keys back?!!! And the longer they would have been in the water, the more damaged they would have become. They were electronic...and then there was a crackhead [insert lightbulb moment HERE]! ...Tuh [Insert bright red hair flip HERE]

#crackheadsforpresident

January 4, 2015 10:38PM - Chicago, IL

Bruh... it is COLD in Chicago. We went to dinner in downtown Chi town and it is 8 degrees. Not 80. Not even 18. MF'N EIGHT DEGREES! Lol lipops and crack rocks it is cold! People willingly live here?! I will NEVER plan a trip to Chicago in the wintertime AGAIN! I'm not about this life... The Moroccan oil in my hair is frozen!

January 5, 2015 7:05AM

Don't ever... EVER complain about ANYTHING until you've slept on a cold airport floor with no jacket bc you wrapped it around your child to keep him warm. & even then he looked up before shivering asleep and said: "mom we're blessed. So we won't complain." GM... Have a great day #strandedinChicago

We were stranded in Chicago. We went to *The Lion King* on Broadway, had dinner at some fancy restaurant (big-ups to Groupon), and made our way to the airport for the flight home only for all end-of-day outgoing flights to be canceled. The temperature had dropped so low that the engines on the planes [at least the smaller ones] wouldn't start. I was heated to say the least. And while the "damsel in distress" acting skills I'd acquired at C.H. Flowers High School deserved an Academy Award for playing the pregnant, single mother with her third child and young son in tow, it would not get us a hotel credit for the night. #iTried. I can't say that it would have mattered, because we definitely were not dressed for the weather. I mean we had just come from the south! There was a two hour wait outside in the cold for a cab. My jeans and leather jacket were no match for the *Windy City* winter. This was before the days of the Uber, and I had yet to learn of Lyft. All of the hotels in a ten-mile radius were sold out—even the ridiculously overpriced hotel above the airport. We were stuck. My phone was dying, the charger was frayed, and broken (thanks Apple), and the stores where I could buy a new one didn't open until early the next morning.

We wandered around the airport until I found a carpeted surface, which happened to be within a windowed hallway. Although it was warmer than most places in the airport, the temperature was still below twenty degrees. I unpacked all of our clothes from our suitcases, both clean and dirty… took off my coat, and wrapped it around my son, and then piled our clothes on top of us. I huddled over him in that cold hallway and the only thing that kept me from crying was that it was too cold to drum up tears.

My son looked up at me and reminded me that we were safe and we had each other. "God loved us and we wouldn't complain." My words. My son was telling his hero *her* words; I was supposed to be saving him, and he was the one who again set my soul at ease. #wedontcomplain

#LUNCHBOXCHRONICLES

Capítulo Tres

#LetTheGrowingBegin
{...Sobre el crecimiento de la flor junto a ella}

January 12, 2015 - Hyattsville, MD
#LunchboxChronicles
Mommy: uhhhhh kid... Where is your lunchbox?!
Kordelle: mommy did you know people in France are dying?!
Mommy: WTF does [that] have to do with your lunchbox?!
Kordelle: I'm just saying... There may be WAY more important things to focus on. (Pauses nervously) Mommy how many weeks are there in a year?
Mommy: sigh. 52. Why?
Kordelle: can I use my piggy bank to buy 52 lunchboxes?

January 14, 2015
#LunchBoxChronicles
Mommy: (ughhhh) do you at least like Beyoncé?!
Kordelle: she's pretty but...So overrated.

Mommy: what?! Pause... You don't like Beyoncé OR JayZ?! What about Biggie? Nas?!
Kordelle: they're ok.
Mommy: get out. You're walking home
Kordelle: why I gotta walk? I brought my lunchbox home!! Fine...
'I'mma call Grandma. She'll come get me. And we'll listen to Tupac.

March 05, 2015 2:09PM - Bowie, MD
#LunchBoxChronicles
(Well not really but still pretty damn funny)
it was Valentine's Day 2015 & Kordelle asked me to take him to Hallmark...
Mommy: but kid I already got your V-day cards for your class
Kordelle: that's not why I wanna go...

Now, being the conceited mother that I am, I started blushing on the inside like "aww my baby wants to buy me a card this year instead of making one!" So I took him. He spent twenty minutes meticulously toiling over the cards to get the perfect one and snatched a small box of chocolates before getting in line. I'm thinking, "I wonder if he knows I'm on a diet?..." I get in line, and reach for the card when it's our turn to pay, only for me to glance at the nature of the card and realized... It wasn't for me. I went ape nuts:

Mommy: aye yo kid... WHO YOU COPPIN THIS CARD FOR?!!!!
WHATS HER NAME?!
Kordelle: mom... Please don't do this...
Mommy: you spent my time and now you bout to spend my money...

'I'MMA NEED A NAME OR 'I'MMA PUT IT ALL BACK- WHATS THE GIRLS NAME?!
Kordelle: (whining) We're in public mom don't do thisssssssssssssssssssss
Mommy: (mommy starts to walk out of line)
Kordelle: ok OK! (Kordelle mumbles some girls name inaudibly)
Mommy: I can't hear you sir speak up please
Kordelle: HER NAME IS SINAYA OK??!
Mommy: (pouts. pays. and tried to get more info but Kordelle doesn't co-operate... Whole line is laughing at us)

the next day now I'm usually a drive by curb side drop off kind of mom but today? Nah. I politely parked the car.
Kordelle: (hella alarmed) Mom... What are you doing?! Mom, ...Don't do this...
Mommy: what ever do you mean babycakes I'm not doing anything
Kordelle: you never park. You never walk me in. MOM YOURE GOING TO EMBARRASS ME
Mommy: I will not! I just wanna walk my little man into class (starts dragging kordelle through the school)
Kordelle: (whining) this isn't going to go wellllllll
Mommy: (we get to his class) NOW WHICH ONE IS SHE?!!!!!
Kordelle: I'm. not. telling. you.
Mommy: that's cool. Bc I swear fo-Gawd I will find out myself! "Which one of yall is Si..."
Kordelle: OK OK CHILL I have to go to school here you know (looks nervous as he points) she's the one in the corner drinking the chocolate milk.

And there she was. This 'lil dark skin cutie with pig tails and glasses. My son was crushing on her. He kicked me out of his classroom, scared that I would embarrass him more. I walked to the car sad AF... I'm not the only woman in my mini's life anymore.

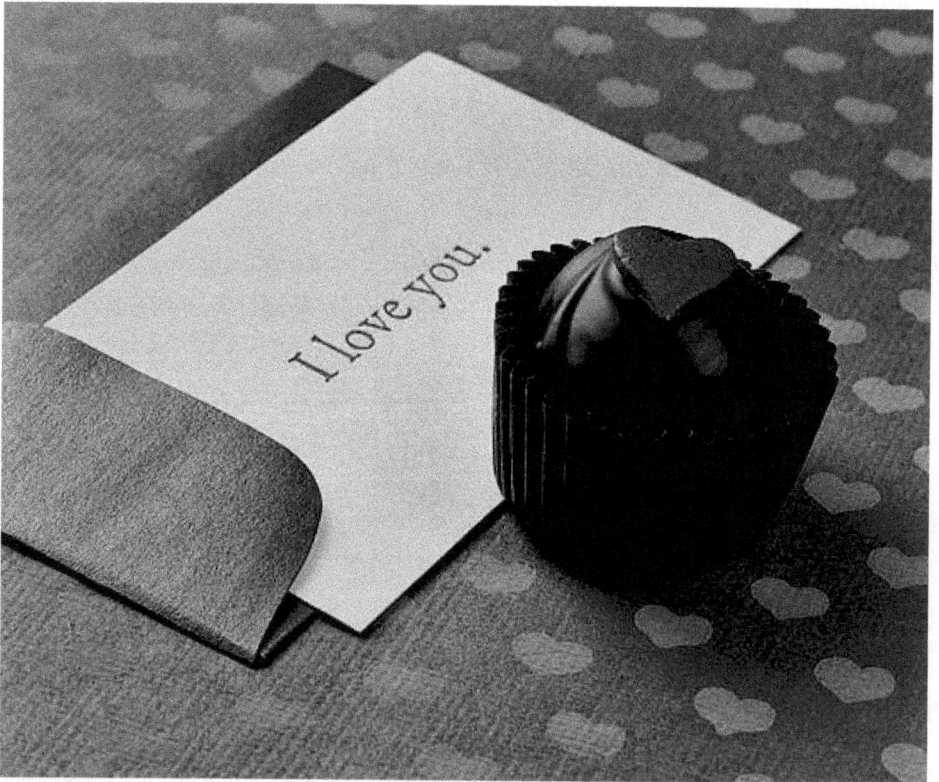

March 12, 2015 7:57am
#LunchBoxChronicles

Every morning I drop my mini off at school. I tell him be smart, learn everything, & if he forgets to bring his lunchbox home he is going to wind up on the side of a milk carton like, "Have you seen this child?" He walks away, turns, & blows me a kiss EVERY morning, no matter who is around. Man I love being a mom...His mom (insert overly gushy face HERE)!

May 10, 2015 1:28PM

(3:52a) kid wakes up with nose bleed...Mom to the rescue!

(4:19a) mom tucks kid in bed with tons of kisses

(4:20a) mom stares at ceiling on couch

(5:41a) mom still stares at ceiling on couch thinking

about all the wrong stuff/people/food...Ughhhhh

My son is a hemophiliac.

Hemophilia (ˌhiːməʊˈfɪlɪə; ˌhɛm-) or hemophilia (pathology) an inheritable disease, usually affecting only males but transmitted by women to their male children, characterized by loss or impairment of the normal clotting ability of blood so that a minor wound may result in fatal bleeding.

I have lost a few jobs because of this. Well, my mouth probably had more to do with the loss of those jobs than anything. We can save that for another book. The effects of hemophilia are far reaching. I have been beyond exhausted on so many days after staying up with him for random uncounted hours in the middle of the night or wee hours of the morning, holding him and his nose until the bleeding stopped and he fell asleep. His nose bleeds were random, happened suddenly with no warning, and there was no true cause. No specialist, test, or explanation ever revealed the geyser that was my son's nose, but stopping the floods were arduous. He would wake up in the middle of the night, covered in blood. Kordelle has been able to catch the bleeding earlier as he has grown older. He started to feel his nose running and he'd jump up. We started keeping tissues by his bedside, and we turned on a vaporizer to decrease the dry air affects. However, nothing ever stopped them. He would go to school tired and exhausted on some days. I would wind up being late to work, as I had one of those jobs that just didn't understand a mother's unexpected life issues and unforeseen occurrences.

Being a massage therapist has taught me innumerable life lessons and maturity. But the biggest lesson I learned while working at Massage Envy was the importance and value of time. Over the years I maintained a disordered, intermittent, energy-altering regimen which enabled me to keep my job. I learned to cope with the effects of my son's condition with coffee, tea, yoga, red wine, and melatonin: the first three to wake me up and the last two to knock me unconscious.

Nights of staying up while my mind wandered, instead of sleeping, began to cause a noticeable problem at work. Even driving to work was cumbersome, as I would fall asleep at the wheel. But in life, there's little room for excuses, and after working there for about four years, in my managers' minds, I had exhausted all of mine.

May 14, 2015 4:38pm - Landover, MD

(I've been so busy all day I didn't have time to update you Walter S. Dyer IV but uhhhh we were lied to)
#LunchBoxChronicles

[side note: semi annoyed I am still able to post these [Lunchbox Chronicles] smh]

Mom: (packing lunch this morning) uhhh Kid... Where's your lunchbox?! ITS NOT IN YOUR BOOKBAG YOU TOLD MR. WALLY YOU DIDNT LEAVE IT AT SCHOOL YOU LIED?!

Kid: no. Ummm apparently I left it at Karate. But I said I didn't leave it at school...So technically I didn't lie.

Mom: what's that have to do with the price of tea in China?!

Kid: you told me that I better not leave my lunchbox at school anymore or I would get a spanking... Well...It's not at school... So...Technically you aren't supposed to spank me...Or then you would be a liar...

Mom: (standing in the kitchen with the WTF face)

Kid: 'I'mma go start the car for you. I'll be in it listening to Tupac if you need me.

I am surrounded by tons of talented people. I know oodles of chefs, artists, photographers, and entrepreneurs. I'm just blessed to live and thrive in an area that is full of just as many successful, driven, and motivated people. My homeboy who I've dubbed in my phone as "W DIV," is addressed by my son as Mr. Wally. One day Mr. Wally (or W DIV) hit me up about doing a photo shoot. We tossed around ideas, and my #TWD (The Walking Dead) obsession at that current moment overtook me. We planned to have a photo shoot in a cemetery around dusk. It was so badass; it was like "pop princess" meets "grunge" meets "Buffy the Vampire Slayer." He brought these super dope guns (unloaded of course) and a balaclava ski mask. I had on make-up, heels, a silver poof dress with a ripped green faded camo jacket. It was dope.

I didn't have anyone to watch Kordelle and that was fine, because as a single mom, I had long ago become accustomed to bringing my son with me to appointments. Thus, over time, I had created a lifestyle that would allow my son to travel with me. My friends all knew him, so it was no surprise to W DIV when I got to the shoot and had the kid. And of course W DIV didn't mind. He even told Kordelle to get in on some of the photos we took (the ones without the guns).

Side note: who knew a shoot at a cemetery was such a great idea?! If they don't do nothing else right with their lives, the property managers sure do make sure that the grass is cut and pristine to a crisp. The sun was shining just right and the trees were abundant and full. The hills were rolling. I'm not sure if the dead people appreciated it, but W DIV and I sure did.

As the shoot was winding down, W DIV asked the kid about his lunch box (as you can see in the post above). But before that, I got my first introduction to "man logic." I'm not a girly girl. Matter of fact, my boyfriend tells me that he sometimes wishes that I was a little less rough around the edges. (I wish he were more romantic, so somehow it all balances out.) By the end of this shoot with me prancing and parlaying around in heels, my feet were TI'D!

I had worked all day and just didn't have any more energy to walk over in the grass where we had finished shooting to get the heels I had changed from, although, it was only about ten feet away. I asked Kordelle if he could get my shoes as we were planning to leave soon.

(Pause)

I looked up and Kordelle had emerged from the car with a pair of sneakers.

(Pause again)

I'm confused because the heels that I had JUST took off were visibly sitting in the grass like…near him.

(Head scratch)

He had to go out of his way to walk to the car to get those sneakers. I asked myself, *How did this make sense to hi*… Never mind, as I interrupted my own confused train of thoughts and instead told him:

"Not those Kordelle. I need the other ones I had earlier. And my bag."

He remerges from the car with the tennis shoes I had gone running with that morning, and a plastic bag that I usually threw them in. Meanwhile my purse and my heels were still sitting in the grass untouched.

(PAUSE! CONFUSED PAUSE!)

W DIV looks up, sees my frustrated face, and yells out, "Hey buddy, go get your mom's heels from the grass along with her purse, and put both of them in the back seat of the car." Kordelle did exactly as he was instructed. I was in awe like, "I just told him to do that!" W DIV looked up from packing his equipment, saw my now extra confused facial expression, and said, "Man logic. You were speaking to him in woman logic. You gotta be direct and specific with us… for everyone's sake. And then don't get upset when we don't get it right the first time because, we're men, we usually don't ever get it right the first time. You gotta start using man logic with him Tai."

May 14, 2015 9:11PM

Eating crab legs with my mini & Scandal comes on. I was asking him about his day and what he did. He asked me if we could talk later because Scandal was coming on. LOL I burst out laughing as he would tune me out in typical man fashion when the football game was on. But I had no idea he had gotten into Scandal. I'm sure I'm going to be in some type of mommy jail for allowing this, but it was a "clean" episode so I sat in awe with him. Man I luh this dude! #watchingScandal #withthekid

May 16, 2015 7:18AM
#LunchBoxChronicles

Kid: mom there's a spider in the bathroom. I'm going to go pee outside.

Mom: Kordelle...There's 5,000 spiders outside. Go back in the bathroom take something with you like a shoe, or something else big and heavy, and kill it.

Kordelle: (picks up his lunchbox as it was closest to him at the time and marches into the bathroom only to run out 30sec later screaming) I've decided that the spider is poisonous and I never have to pee again it's his bathroom now.

Mom: (I go into the bathroom) Kordelle...It's a daddy long leg.

#LUNCHBOXCHRONICLES

Capítulo Quatro

#Transitions

{...Sólo crece}

May 17, 2015 - Capital Heights, MD

Yo. I swear looking for a house to buy is like dating. You compile lists of the perfect house to call Home with all the things you want to have in your house; at the end of the day you're still left to choose from what's available at the moment on the market for sale. & you'll never find that perfect house- unless you build & mold it. Of which takes time. & money & patience. Just like finding a spouse: time, money & patience & they still won't be perfect. & you build a list of men...I mean houses that you want. & you may like 4 or 5 different houses but you can only commit to one. So you make final cuts & you go to put an offer in on it but someone else has already claimed it bc your timing was off & the "for sale" sign is replaced with an "off the market" sign & you try not to get your feelings hurt even though you fell in love with THAT person...I mean house, they wind up settling & closing with someone else. & the other houses you scratched off your lists have now been claimed by other people. & you start over from nothing... Search- ing for happiness with these empty lists. Hoping the perfect house will find you. Sheesh... I need a drink. This is like emotional deja vu #househunting #housechronicles

May 21, 2015 4:33AM
Kid wakes me up & he's covered in blood. I'm like "ZOMBIE APOC- OLYPSE IS UPON US?!" No...Just a nose bleed. Smh, #TWD has changed me forever. Now? I can't sleep its cool. Its overrated anyways. But that totally means I get COFFEE in the morning.

June 04, 2015 8:16AM
So...Taime Out Massage Studios has been invited for career day to tell your children all about the wonderful world of massage. Wish I had known back in the second-grade that career options extended further than firefighter, teacher, and doctor... Would've made my life much easier in the future, & THEY GAVE ME COFFEE ITS GOING TO BE A GREAT DAY.

Visiting my son's school to speak to students for career day was like hitting an occupational reset button. In front of scholarly crowds, my soapbox platform, and social reform, I birthed a campaign to change minds—the wave of our survival is through our youth. While speaking to the kids, gathering their feedback, and gauging how their minds viewed the future I realized we raise our kids all wrong.

It didn't dawn on me until recently, but we are cyclically doing it all wrong. The subliminal messages we are passing on to our children speak death into their futures—glass ceilings and elongated retirement dates, with hopeful pensions and social security checks that may not even be there when they turn sixty-five. "Train up a child in the way he should go, and when he is old he will not depart from it." (Proverbs 22:6)

No wonder we have a world so full of followers who are immune to thinking for themselves, because that's how we raise them! And from that, they'll never stray.

Growing up, I vividly remember my parents telling me that it was my job to go to school, to get good grades so that I could get a good job. To GET a good job.

/get/

verb

1. be given, presented with, or paid (something): "most businesses will get a tax cut" synonyms: be presented with, be awarded, collect, garner, receive

2. to come to have or hold; suffer, experience, or be subject to (specified treatment)

In the very definition it eludes to waiting... no allowing someone else to bestow something upon you even after you've earned it! And in doing so, we allow another person (or people) to dictate and decide our worth. You are worth $15 an hour. That's it? You are worth $60 and hour. That's it? And why are we personally content with embracing a dollar amount for our time and worth per hour?; the problem therein lies that we allow SOMEONE ELSE to set that price.

Malcolm X, in his earlier years of describing black-nationalism, described that the black man will never be in control of his community if he does not control his commerce. Fast forward for a moment before Sankofa-ing back in time to when the revolution was real; we have lost complete control. In us fighting to be equal, we gave over control of our schools, our churches, our stores, our markets; sold our souls to sit at *their* tables and drink from *their* fountains. See, during the flourishing period of

Black Wall Street, blacks were thriving. Not just surviving or existing as we see today, but I mean *thriving*. Not because they wanted to, but because they had to.

While we did not have access to white schools, white hospitals, white markets, we were forced to create our own. From the early 1900s well in to 1930, African American communities flourished with early entrepreneurs. In these communities, during prohibition and right before the Great Depression, the dollar circulated thirty-six to 100 times often taking almost up to a year for it to leave the community. A study highlighted in *Black Wall Street: A Lost Dream* by Jay Jay Wallace and Dr. Ron Wallace, English and Poetry Professor at The University of Wisconsin-Madison, notes that the dollar now leaves the black community within fifteen minutes.

With every black dollar that leaves the community goes a say so in how that dollar will be spent...the laws that are created, buildings erected, political officials elected, police officers sworn in. That dollar is powerful, but only amongst those with the power. Regain control of our commerce thus we regain control of our communities. The only way fathomable to do that is not to enter through the back door and cry reparation pleas hoping to receive handouts and better laws—NO! We regain control by entering through the front door, kicking it in with an NWA vengeance and reclaiming what we sold away decades ago. We do that by educating our youth properly to create a better future, the future from which we walked away.

In light of our truth, what do I teach every child I come into contact with? To create.

"What do you want to CREATE when you grow up?"

I replace the projected foreshadowing on our young kings and queens with a future full of hope and tenacity that is not filled simply with faith that *if I try hard enough…* Their mindsets shift from "if" to "when."

"Your job is to go to school, to make good grades, to MAKE a good job."

Us colored folk sat at the countertops until the hounds were sent in. We were water-whipped with the hoses. Beaten in the streets like rabid dogs, praying and singing old negro spirituals for equality and peace. And then one day… it happened. I mean, not overnight. But eventually, we overcame (sort of). And we stopped creating and started settling. We stopped dreaming and starting existing. A mixture of American pride conjured with two centuries of inferiority filled our homes; those seats that we were told (for so long) that we could not have were seats that we now embodied… but it was at a cost. We traded our Black Wall Streets for American capitalism. Oh to be an American. Stop subscribing to dated capitalistic regimes, turn to your children, and encourage them to dream.

Some of my most stressed out clients make the most money. It is never about money. Rich people commit suicide all the time, and celebrities walk around with a comma'd bank account and empty spirits. If you do what makes you happy, you'll never work a day in your life. To do what makes you happy, you will not only have to be in touch with reality, but you must also be in touch with yourself. Knowing self is the quickest direct route to happiness. Once you are happy, you have a much more rational and clear mind to achieve wealth.

I often turn to my stressed-out clients and ask them to go back with me. "Go back to when you were in the second grade. Had a pack of crayons in one hand and a pencil in the other. A blank paper on your desk and were instructed by the teacher to draw a picture of what you wanted to be when you grew up."

My clients close their eyes and revert back to that day (we all have one). I interrupt their thoughts and ask them, "What picture did you draw?" They give me all kinds of answers. And it never fails—the answers are not tied to what made sense; what made them money; what made them successful. They were solely based on what made them happy. Now in our grown-up minds if we did the same exercise—allowed ourselves to dream—our life experiences and exposure to occupations and passions that stem further than the standard "doctor/lawyer/dancer/teacher" would yield careers based around happiness. We dream in happiness.

My son came home a few days before I was to speak at his school and announced that he had created a brand-new business. I turned the radio off and said, "Oh really baby? Tell me all about it!" I was so proud of my mini me. He was dreaming. And not only did he think it up, he wrote it down, and put a plan into action. My son loved to draw. And because he had a tomboy mommy for a mama, he also had a shoe addiction. Attending school in one of the richest black counties in America, he was amongst several other entitled young black children who also embraced societal norms of the latest and greatest. Thus, my son saw an opportunity and implemented one of the teachings I ran around the house saying, "See a need, fill a need."

He started drawing shoe designs for kids at his school. Each basic shoe design was a quarter; it came in black and white and they were subjected to whatever design he wanted to give them. But if they wanted a more personalized design, they would book an appointment after school and he would spend quality time creating a customized shoe design for $1. It was in full color and tailored to their needs.

I was floored at how deeply he had thought this through! He then showed me his business plan and how he was going to recruit and market more business: his karate after-care program serviced three schools in the surrounding areas. He was going to create coupons for the kids that went to the other schools, and set up a shoe design stand on the corner in the middle of all three schools in the summer time.

Kordelle explained to me that no one knew what kids liked better than a fellow kid. He had an employee list, and even told me he made his best friend his apprentice. I made him spell it. I refused to let my son use words that he didn't know how to spell. He showed his friend, the apprentice, how to make the shoe designs in a similar manner. He had an "employee manual" portraying the pay scale, and his only rule was, "NO FREE WORK." When he was done explaining his company to me, he showed me his first marketing ad, and asked if he could use the copy machine once we got home to make duplicates.

I was speechless. I was even more speechless when he opened up his hand and showed me $5.25 he had collected for his first day's work. I asked him what he wanted for dinner and to Subway we headed; (without paying taxes on his earnings. Shhhh don't tell the IRS).

I supported my baby's dream so much, and I wanted to offer a foundation for his growth. While I had no idea if the concept already existed (I'm sure it does), Kordelle was right: kids do know what kids like. Since everything is impossible until it is done, I contacted Nike and pitched to them the idea of Kordelle working with them over the summer to design high performance kids sneakers. Still waiting to hear back from Nike.

June 04, 2015 8:24AM
#LunchboxChronicles
Mommy: (walking to the car locking the house door) Kid... It's cold outside do you want a jacket?

Kid: no. I'm fine. I'm a man a little cold doesn't bother me.

Mommy: fine. You better not get sick because I'm NOT taking you to a hospital! (Insert pause as I drive down the street) CRAP! I left my cell phone charger I need to go back.

Kid: cool. When you do can you get my lunch box? I left it on the bed. AND BEFORE YOU YELL...There's no rules or spanking promises in play of me leaving it at home! I'm sorry, you're the best mom ever.

Mom: (feeling manipulated, turn back around to go get charger and lunchbox)

Kid: oh & since you're already heading back in... Can you get my jacket too? Thanks. Love you.

June 04, 2015 9:14AM

YO... THESE KIDS ARE RUTHLESS!

"How much does a massage cost?"

"Why do you charge so much?"

"I thought we couldn't go to Cuba? Wait... Jay Z went to Cuba. You know Jay Z?"

"Where is your spa at?"

"How much money do you make?"

"Your boss let you dye your hair purple? Does it go into your brain?!"

"How many naked people do you see a day?"

"Wait... You don't have a boss? So you get to do what you want?! I want to be a massage therapist!"

"Since I'm half the size of an adult will my massage cost half the price?"

"Do they have massages on the moon?" (Apparently I went after an astronaut)

And then the one that got me was:
"so... You go to someone's house to do the massage and they pay you? How do you get your money? Wait...What do you do if someone doesn't pay you? What if they don't have any money but you already gave them the massage?"
...the astronaut aint get none of these effin questions.

I honestly didn't have an answer to a good amount of those questions. I was standing in the line of fire being full blown attacked by stimulated second graders about my life, and I should have known the answers, but I didn't! And these were some good questions! Like, what was I going to do if I massage someone and they do not have any funds? *Smack them out like Rihanna in her video #BBHMM? I didn't have a kitchen to bury them in, making unpaying patrons wash dishes 'til their debts were square; I mean I could put them in their kitchen but it wouldn't have the same effect. Do I call the cops?* I needed to research this.

June 12, 2015
(Mommy falls off the couch... Stumbles in the kid's room to wake him up)

Mommy: oh... You're up already. And...Dressed. Umm...Ok. Thanks.
Kid: (twiddling his thumbs) SOOooo. Missy. What kept you in the bed so late?
Mommy: Tiffany *came over last night.*
Kid: oh. I thought you were going to blame it on the two empty bottles of wine by the couch.
Mommy: (crickets) I'm going to go lay back down. My head hurts. You're buying lunch today btw.

Kid: GREAT!... Because I don't know where my lunchbox is.

Mommy: Kordelle WTF?! Stop being so irresponsible dammit!

Kid: (mumbling really low) says

She with a hangover on a Friday morning.

Mommy: wth did you just say?! I heard something! (I didn't figure it out til later)

Kid: I said you're the bestest mommy. go lay back down, I'll get you up in an hr.

Mommy: (deciding whether to attempt to smack the black off the kid just because... or go get a Tylenol)... Ok.

You know how you don't hear something right away? It has to take time to register? It registered about 2min after I dropped him off at school. It's cool. I'll have the smack waiting for him this afternoon. It'll be good and marinated. And sober.

June 15, 2015

Soooooooo... Whennnnnn do you have "the talk"? Because he def just asked me what's sex.

June 17, 2015

Currently getting fussed at. For using all the batteries that he needs for his toys. That I bought with my money. For my stuff. Funny how that works please hold (insert Kordelle continuing to spazz HERE).

June 20, 2015

#LunchBoxChronicles

(I wanted to share a message that Jehovah encouraged me to share with this man)

It had been raining relentlessly for a few days. It seemed to be raining even harder by the time I got off of work each day. But I was tired of giving my son lunch money because I was too lazy to go to the grocery store to buy food for his lunch. But then again, I'm not even sure if that was the real reason to be honest, because the way my natural hair is set up, rain and humidity are pure kryptonite. But I suppose eating trumps edges.

June 22, 2015

Coming out of the grocery store this man asked if I needed help with my groceries. Usually I'm supermom & I say no but I took one look at the rain & said yes. However, I informed him ahead of time I didn't have any change on me. He said "oh well I just want a little change to eat." I understandingly apologized & told him I didn't have any, and motioned to where my vehicle was parked. He said, "ok..." And turned from me to the next shopper coming out.

I went & loaded my car...In the pouring rain...Annoyed. God talked to me & I listened & even more importantly obeyed in the message I was told to give.

I returned my cart, grabbed a box of protein bars, & went back to the man. Introduced myself & said I was a Child of God. & told him that doing the right thing should not be governed by what someone can do for you. You should do it because it's the right thing to do. Instead of working for the wealth of the world you should instead sow into His kingdom. You knew I needed help & chose to ignore me because I couldn't do anything for you, God told me to tell you that He loves you & wants to use you if you let Him. I gave him the box of food. He started crying & thanked me. I told him thank God, I didn't do anything.

Evangelism isn't just knocking on someone's door demanding they love God, and it isn't even going to church every week. It's living the blessings. Your works are how you spread His word. Do what's right not because someone is watching or because you'll be paid for it... But just because it's the right thing to do. & allow Him to use you. Imagine the change we can create. #Agape

Often, I infuse core values into my son that I see missing among adults, mainly men who are interested in me. When I correct others, I usually take the position that, "I have one man to raise. I don't have time for two." or "He grown, I'm not in the business of raising grown folk." But over the years through maturity and allowing my own discernment to develop, I am humbled in the lessons I share with grown-ups and children alike. If we are all children of God, and it takes a village to raise a child, that tutelage does not cease just because that child reaches a certain age on paper. I now pick and choose my battles, but with God's assistance, I allow lessons to flow through me to others no matter their age.

I use to become annoyed that certain lessons evaded the masculine masses, but again, in my maturity and humility, I have realized how many life lessons that I missed. I would question, "How did you make it to 34, 35, 36 years of age and don't know how to treat a lady?" Same way any of us miss life lessons… we just do. When my faith and discernment are on point, I stop and pour out whatever God would like me to pass along. Frequently, we assume it is somebody else's responsibility to teach or encourage or educate someone (both young or old), but what if that somebody is you? I am my brother's + my father's + my uncle's + my son's keeper. I have a direct responsibility to maintain the cultural thermostat of the world in which I live. Whether it's picking up a piece of paper or an empty can, I pass on the street, being still and slowing my pace for a man in front of me to open a door, or educating someone to be loving just to be loving, without any strings attached—I have a part to play.

June 25, 2015
#LunchboxChronicles

Mommy: Kordelle. WHY IS YOUR LUNCHBOX IN SHREDDED PIECES?!
Kordelle: but... I brought it home.
Mommy: but it's in shambles! TF happened?!
Kordelle: I don't know.
Mommy: what do you mean you don't know?! It's YOUR lunchbox!
Kordelle: ummm... Things happen you know. I'm sorry mommy.
Mommy: BUT ITS IN PIECES KORDELLE
Kordelle: school is over I don't need it anymore.
Mommy: kid. You have summer camp.
Kordelle: oh. Truuuuu. well. There's always duct tape. The airplane mechanics use it!
(Kordelle opens a drawer & slides mommy duct tape)

July 04, 2015 6:23PM - Atlanta, GA
I don't know if I can say it enough... & I don't care if anyone gets tired of hearing it: omg I LOVE being a mom! This kid is just dope!

July 04, 2015 9:26PM
Ameir (my homegirl's kid): I lost Kordelle
Me: tf you mean you lost him?!
Ameir: I dunno. He's just gone.
Me: wayment what? Ameir if you don't go find my tax write off YOURE

GUNNA COME UP MISSING!

Ameir: I don't get it

Me: go find KC!

Ameir: but I didn't lose him he lost himself!

(Kordelle comes out the bathroom) Bruh is a certified ninja when tf did he even pass me?!

July 04, 2015 9:43PM

My tax write off is trippin. Kordelle is begging me for a pet owl. Tasha come get your friend.

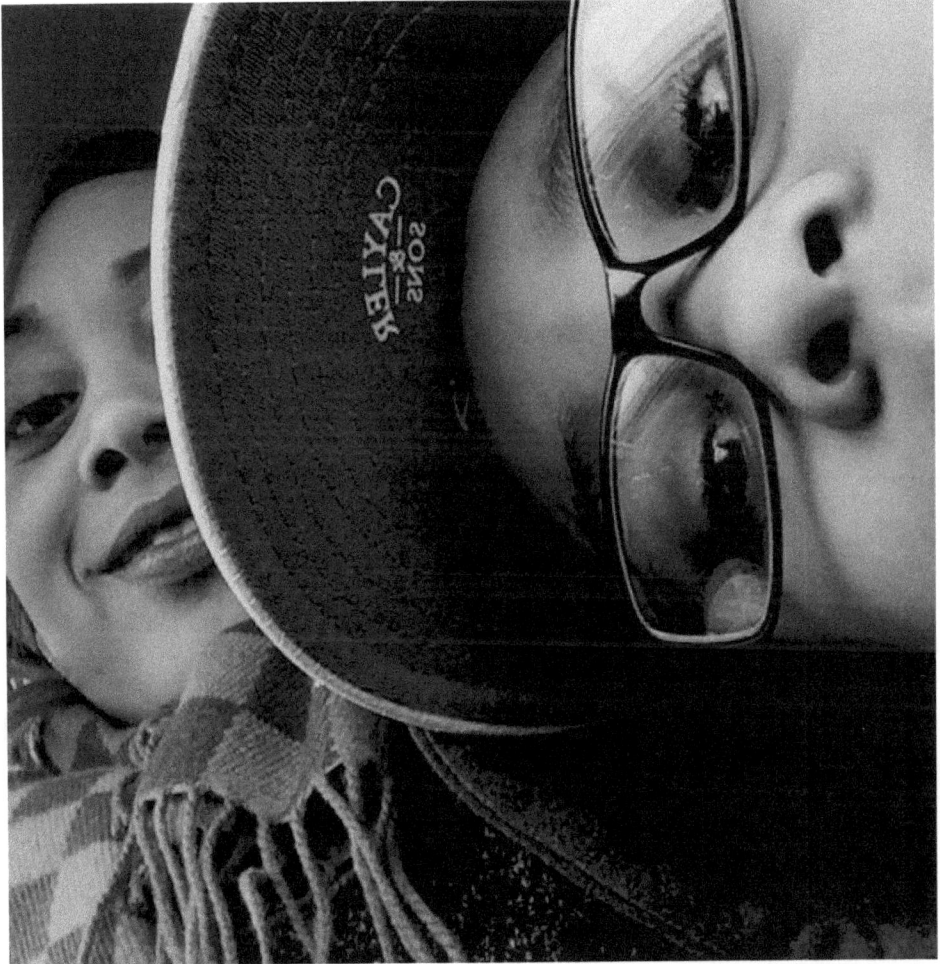

#LUNCHBOXCHRONICLES

Capítulo Cinco
#Baltimore
{Botón de Rearranque}

Mid-Summer 2015: Havana

I was in Cuba—illegally—trying NOT to get deported back to America as I watched my soon-to-be new neighborhood in Baltimore burn via a shabby green and black small tube television in the streets of Havana. The natives could barely get Wi-Fi but had somehow managed to keep up with the current riots happening in Baltimore, Maryland.

It was Trayvon Martin all over again. Standing in the streets of the largest decrepit Caribbean Island brought back the feeling I had when I was living in Thailand and the "not-guilty" verdict was delivered on the Zimmerman Case.

I had spent some time in South East Asia learning Thai massage, away from any form of normality I had come to know. I was the only black student and single mom enrolled in a school full of foreigners from around the world. I remember the clamminess that ran across my palms; the blood leaving my face. I remember the instant dry throat sensation as if I had been screaming for hours though I was left utterly speechless as I watched my country let me down again. I remember how cranky I was for the remain der of that day in Chiang Mai. I was unable to pinpoint exactly why 'til one of my Canadian Caucasian classmates mentioned the case, and then questioned over dinner after noting my sour mood, "Well did you know the family or something?"

Blackness is unexplainable. No matter how close or far-removed you may *think* you are, it's engrained in our melanin to feel century old setbacks and deep-rooted cultural pain. This is especially true for national pain which is a blatant reminder—even with decades of old spirituals, negro hymns, and protests behind us. Maybe we ain't really overcame as much as we thought.

In hindsight, the Baltimore riots were the best and the worst thing that could have happened to the city in the past decade. It brought attention to the racial tensions that swarm throughout the neighborhoods; disparity that filled B-more towns like a silent deadly gas that invaded the downtown high-rise buildings, and filled the nostrils of the homeless men begging for change on the sidewalks right below. This deadly contaminate has circulated through the ignored hacks by the people passing them by. The racial tension roamed the crime riddled projects with a clear line between the haves and have nots—with brownstone homes on one side of the street and projects on the other.

The riots highlighted how derelict the boarded rowhomes are, and how considerably neglected the city has become. A problem for most, but a gold mine for developers who came in drones to run down inner-city neighborhoods high in potential…they began to purchase as much property as they could get their hands on for the low, fixed them up for the low, and then sold them to the highest buyer. Fast forward two years later and I saw white people moving into my neighborhood. I knew the stench aroma of gentrified capitalism packaged in thin lipped, straight hair—eight hundred plus credit scores were upon us.

#Baltimore

The looming gentrification that began to hover over the city became sickening. Just like many East Coast cities, Baltimore has more renters per capita than owners. The cyclical mentality that is passed down from generation to the next is to rent, not own, making it a piece of cake for native Baltimoreans to be pushed out of the neighborhoods they have called "home" for several decades now.

Everyone looks good. Everyone sports various name brands. Everyone seeks to maintain nice cars, nice shoes, nice purses. They collect things that depreciate in value and many invest little in assets. While the riots were temporary, the attention that it brought to the city, MY city, is soon going to change the town forever.

You cannot stop the ball of change once it gets rolling; you either get with it or you'll get run over. While in Cuba, I foreshadowed the socioeconomic divide that would transform Baltimore into a booming metropolis greater than DC. Baltimore's ports are larger and closer to northern shores—bringing in more seafood, sailing out more cruise ships. Paralleled in ideology, I devised a plan to infuse progressive thinking skills into my mini.

Midsummer 2015 - Hyattsville, MD

"Can I have two dollars? "Kordelle asked.
"For what?" I replied.
"Just because I want to buy this game, and I am two dollars short" Kordelle said.
"What did you do to earn these two dollars?"

I didn't care what he wanted the money for to be honest. I wanted to know what he had done to earn it. Nothing in this world is free. I continued instilling in him values about money. He knew the freedom it afforded. But now he was more than old enough to embrace the responsibilities associated with it. I told him that his job was to go to school to get good grades to make a good job. Just like mommy had a job description for her career, he too had a job description.

Kordelle wrote out thirty-two things as a part of his job description. However, he does not receive extra payment for things that are expected of him. Cleaning his room, making good grades, taking out the trash, sweeping the kitchen floor, washing the dishes—they were already included in his payment that he received daily, a roof over his head, food on the table, and a ride to school each morning. If he wanted two extra dollars, a "bonus," we shall call it, he had to go above and beyond his normal job description to earn his bonus.

Kordelle picked up trash in front of our apartment building. He fed the feral cats. He helped me pack boxes of clothes for our pending move. And he carefully wrapped three sets of wine glasses. When we had finished, I gave him ten dollars. He had worked so hard for his ten bucks that he actually didn't want to spend it. Earlier that year around his birthday, Kordelle had asked for a credit card. I instead hand rolled all of his piggy bank change with him over the course of three days, took him to the bank, and opened a savings account depositing all of the change into the account. It was a little over $120.

Kordelle asked me if I could take his original $8 as well as his newly earned $10 and deposit it into his savings account. He told me that he would save all of it for college and his own house one day. He helped me pack a few more boxes before we ordered pizza and watched *Black-ish* together.

July 14, 2015
#HouseChronicles

so... Who wants to hear a funny story? Bought a house. Yayy go me. AND I have a college degree so you would think I would know better right? Nope. I go to change the alarm codes bc I was never given instructions & see three names. I change the name & code for the first 2, & the third one I changed the code but when I went to change the name from "Duress" (I had been pronouncing it as "Doris) it wouldn't let me. So after putting in that particular code several times to change it, I gave up & let it be. My friend & I are about to leave when banging starts on the door & in bursts this FIONE cop. I thought we were getting robbed when my homegirl Taja reminded me people usually don't knock before they rob you. My 2nd thought: one of my friends sent me a stripper as a housewarming present!

Then in comes a taller even more fine officer with a gun & light; said he was about to break down the back door but when he heard laughing he decided to come in the front. We're all confused when cop #1 says "you called us." I'm like, "aint nobody call you! My phone is dead!" He says, "no. On your security alarm system." "Duress"...Is not a name. In my defense it blended in with the other names. I paused & realized the cops had gotten there in 3min. I said, "oh you must've thought I was white huh?!" Good to know that not only does the silent panic alarm feature work, Baltimore's finest is literally FINE. I asked him if he was sure he wasn't sent to strip for me. I got my own handcuffs...They smirked & bid me goodnight. (I watched his butt as he walked away #creeplife)

August 03, 2015
Writing the FULL rules for the lunchbox this year. I'm trying to remember all the excuses he used during the lunchbox chronicles; Kordelle won't catch me slipping 2015-16 school year!

August 19, 2015 3:23PM - Providence, RI
(I hear off in the distance...)

Kid: have you seen a woman version of me with blue hair... Almost the same height?
Zoo person: she went that way by the moon bear
(No she didn't she's behind you!)
Me: no kid wait here I am!
Kid: (taking off in the wrong direction) THANKS MR!
...Ughhhhhhhh

August 19, 2015 6:42PM
About to go watch the sun set atop of mansions in Newport, Rhode Island. #ilovemylife

August 20, 2015
My son has turned into a mini motivational guru trying to convince me to get me on this wall... Bruh... The way gravity is set up ...

I think we had made our way up through what I had dubbed "The New Englands." This particular trip was inclusive of Connecticut, Rhode Island, Massachusetts, New Hampshire, and Vermont. And somewhere along the way, my son developed a love for rock climbing. I think he picked it up last year when we were in Nebraska.

Rock climbing is similar to riding a bike, no matter how much time has passed since you last rode, you never forget how to ride; it comes right back to you. Once you've figured out the art of rock climbing, it comes right back to you. Well, all of those times I was just his cheerleader, I never actually climbed with him…'til this one time on a hot day in August in a humid city somewhere in Massachusetts. And the kid got to a part of the wall where he couldn't climb. He tried so hard and I was trying my best to encourage him when he came up with this insanely bright idea, "Mommy, why don't you show me how to do it?!"

He turned into a modern-day Farrah Gray with a dash of Iyanla Vanzant. (Smh) the things I do for this kid. I put on climbing gear that felt very much like a Velcro diaper, got halfway up the wall and was like, "Nope. I like my life. But I like it much better on the ground." And right when I looked down and was about to release to float back to earth I noticed who was watching. And how proud he was. My hands and calves were burning. My fingertips were numb. My quads hated me. But I kept going up. I made it to the top and he cheered so loud. I floated down (it wasn't as graceful as they make it look. It was more like controlled flailing). Next thing I know my son had run up the same area of the wall where he struggled before. He reached the top in no time and then floated back down as well, way more graceful than I had. I was pretty impressed and asked him, "How did you get up that fast that time?" He told me that he saw how I placed my feet and turned my body to the side of the wall where he had been. He watched me hug the wall and he did the same thing. It's amazing that while we may be parents, our children help us to fully grow up. While I mold him, he molds me right back in return.

August 21, 2015 8:02AM - Boston, MA
DID YOU KNOW PLYMOUTH ROCK IS IN MASSACHUSETTS?! 'I'mma go land on it!

August 21, 2015 11:55AM
Boy Wonder is messing up my agenda! I SHOULD HAVE LANDED ON PLYMOUTH BY NOW. But no. He's still sleep.

I landed. And I must say, Plymouth Rock actually wasn't that impressive. Real talk… it's just a rock. A simple, underwhelming, basic rock. I expected so much more from you Plymouth. Don't let them fool you, size does matter.

August 22, 2015 8:01PM
Rock Climbing. Laser Tag. Hiking. & this kid wants to add canoeing on before breakfast? My body hurts #NewHampshireBound

August 22, 2015 5:19PM
BONUS STATE! (Ran out of stuff to do in New Hampshire... No seriously it's the most boring state we've ever been to we'll come back in the winter and do a whale watching cruise) #VermontBound

Vermont Vermont Vermont. What can I say? Montpelier was breathtaking. The lakes; the mountains with their ice snow caps; the meadows and dew drops were wet morning kisses across the curling land. It looked like the screensavers of which I grew up daydreaming my life away. Oh, and everyone stares but doesn't speak. I understand at the time my hair was blue and while that may not be the norm there…or anywhere for that matter…I don't think they were staring because my hair was blue, but more so, because our skin was brown.

As we have been making our way across the forty-eight contiguous states (we'll get to Hawaii and Alaska eventually), I have been slowly "waking my son up." Part of my frustrations with him and his lunch box aren't solely because I get tired of constantly replacing his lunch box. But it's indicative of how oblivious he is to his surroundings and his person. And that downright scares me. A young black child growing up in the twenty-first century where being black is punishable by death—cops shoot first and ask questions later—I cannot afford for my child to not know what is going on around him.

I'm just not strong enough for that. My love isn't arranged that way, I am NOT built Ford tough to last. If anything were to ever happen to my son, I would crumble.

My heart breaks for the moms I've seen on television interviewing after their sons were killed at the hands of police. I find myself crying with them and I never even knew their kids! I stopped shielding him from the world and coddling him in the overprotective quarters of Prince George's County in hopes that enamoring him with an armor of knowledge, even at such a young age, would create a foundation of protection and awareness.

As we made our way through the valleys, stopping at gas stations and local attractions, the glares and gazes became more apparent. He picked up on it and said, "Mommy I think they're staring at your hair!" I curtly responded in correction, "No baby, they're staring at your skin." He simply responded, "Oh." Every time we have one of those encounters or heavy weighted discussions about racism and discrimination I feel like I am robbing him of his innocence.

Hatred, racism, and fear are taught and acquired. They are not innate. Living in the North has afforded us several luxuries, one of which was the pseudo-security in that we are free. We have mixed schools, upscale restaurants, thriving job opportunities, non-dilapidated hospitals. But maybe that freedom I thought we had was the veil that W.E.B. Du Bois referred to a century prior to the world snatching Trayvon Martin's or Mike Brown's freedom away.

Freedom is a very pliable word that is thrown around too loosely. It falls in the category of "Love" or "Life," and other words that have no true definition. There is no real demarcation of 'free' in the land that has been dubbed "The Land of the Free." Perhaps I missed the small print at the end of that disclaimer that reads, "Only if you are white."

When we were in Texas, I tried my hardest not to stop, but the gas tank made me. We were in Waco. My son hopped out of the rental and obliviously Diddy Bopped his way into the gas station skipping through the aisles looking for Pringles, his snack addiction at the time. I made my way to checkout and hesitantly slid a twenty (dollar bill) across the counter to the man, as their antiquated pumps didn't take credit cards.

Without batting an eye or skipping a beat, the man replied to me never looking up from his paper, "We don't take too well to your kind round these parts. You best gets on." He kicked his overall'ed pant leg up perching his edema filled left ankle on his right knee, flipped the page of the news column, and kept reading.

Not once did we make eye contact, but we didn't need to. I made eye contact with his shot gun sitting next to the register—a rusted sawed-off that looked like it definitely still worked. I thanked the man and hollered for Kordelle to leave the store; "Kordelle let's go!" Kordelle whined in return, "But mom I didn't find any Pringles yet." He instead grabbed a plain bag of Lays chips, scurried to the counter placing his merchandise alongside his money in front of the man.

The man looked at the food and snatched it away hollering back, "I told you to take your monkey and git!" Kordelle was so confused as I had been teaching him about money. He was learning the value of a dollar and knew that money allowed him to buy the things that he wanted. At that moment, he wanted the chips; he provided the money…the confused look on his face spoke, "You have the chips; I have the money, why can't we switch?"

I was too terrified to lecture him about talking back, or to stop mid fear, induced with adrenaline to rush to explain the situation. I snatched my heart by his arm and ran out of that gas station faster than a sinner at a saints' convention. Tossed him in the passenger side of the car, peeled out the parking lot like Danica Patrick, and didn't say a word for the next five minutes fighting back tears. Kordelle finally asked me why we left before we got chips. There was a Caucasian family riding bikes along the sidewalk. I asked Kordelle to look at them, and tell me what he saw: "How are they different than us?" He named everything under the sun from the fact that their family had a daddy, they had a dog, the kid had a shiny red bike unlike his green one with training wheels. The mom had long black hair. He addressed everything except for their skin color. With no sugar coat or sweetness in my response, I told him exactly what happened.

He sat quietly and listened. And all he said when I was done was "Oh." I asked him if he had any questions.

"No. I get it."

We drove to the next gas station one town over in silence on faith and gas fumes praying we didn't break down in Waco.

That wasn't our first encounter with racism and it wouldn't be our last. All I knew was that our black boys were being hunted. We're prey, sleeping cattle at night, unaware of the looming civil war. While I kept stating, "Kordelle I need you to come home with your lunch box." The severity of him being born black translated my request to, "Kordelle I need you to come home alive."

There was a huge problem that wasn't being addressed in this country like the pink elephant in the room—the elephant had just gotten bold and belligerent. Had invited himself to dine, seated at the helm of the country's dinner table, and wasn't leaving anytime soon. Black culture is looking around at all the non-minorities, "Soooooo... we not going to talk about this elephant? Just going to...sit here like there isn't a ridiculous disrespectful large pink elephant eating us out of house and home? Oh aiite."

Now fast forward a year and thousands of miles away in Vermont. Those same feelings started to arise. But here, it was different. No one said anything crude or mean. They just stared. Having to be overly conscious of how I acted and what I said, knowing the world was watching, and this may have been the only time they would encounter black people aside from what they see on TV felt much like being on Broadway under bright lights. Except I didn't have a check waiting for me in my dressing room.

We went to Ben and Jerry's Waterbury Factory, tried way too many different flavors, and allowed the sugar rush to take us away before heading to the beach. While I know there are black people in Vermont, I will say I wasn't saddened to decrease that number by two when we left. I don't think I am a control freak, while some of my acquaintances and ex boyfriends may disagree, but knowing what's going on around me gives me a sense of peace. The entire time we were in Vermont during that hot summer, I had no peace. I had faith and fear.

#LUNCHBOXCHRONICLES

Capítulo Seis
#DontTryJustDo
{Hay una primera vez para todo}

August 25, 2015
*YOU GOTTA BE EFFIN KIDDING ME?!!!! It's the first damn day of
school bruh! We just talked about this! And yet in still...#LunchboxChron-
icles*

*Mommy takes off half a day to make sure the kid is situated for his first day
of school. Drops kid off. Realizes I have time to take a nice 2hr nap before
work. Drives ALL the way back to Baltimore. Gets out the car, looks in the
backseat...and sees a shiny brand new red lunchbox. Bc of an accident I
have to drive IN traffic 90min back to kid's school to take him food. There
goes my nap smfh.*
I quit. And its day 1.

August 30, 2015 - Baltimore City, MD
#LunchboxChronicles
Kid: mommy can I have a job
Mommy: you have a job. your job is to go to school and get good grades.
Kid: yeaaaaaa...but that doesn't pay money
Mommy: but it will one day
Kid: yeaaaaaa...but I need one that does now
Mommy: why?
Kid: I kinda sorta maybe just a little but not much actually there's a high possibility that I could have lost my lunchbox but I'm not completely all the way sure. it could just be you know...invisible.
Mommy: (crickets)...(crickets)...insert mommy spazzing HERE
Kid: hey mommy...how many cell phones did you go through last year?
Mommy: (pause...wait for it...wait for ittttt) SPAZZING "GTFOH ARE YOU EFFIN KIDDING ME I AM AN ADULT I PAY BILLS I HAVE A JOB I CAN LOSE AS MANY DAMN PHONES AS I WANT!"
Kid: ...that's why I asked you for a job 5 minutes ago ma

I tell the kid it's my job to go to work and make money. It allows me to pay him for doing his job. He knows his job is to go to school and make good grades. I reminded him of his (already assigned) job and that his payment for doing his job is that I feed him, clothe him, keep the utilities on, and even reward him with a little bit of cable television.

As I mentioned before, I don't believe in rewarding kids for things they are supposed to do, even though my parents definitely paid me for my grades (lol). My dad would give me five dollars for every A, one dollar for every B, punishment and chores for C's, and I would contemplate running away for anything else. Straight A's would get us dinner at the restaurant of my choice.

But yea, I'm not my dad. I look just like him, but our bank accounts are set up differently. Matter fact, I started threatening to stop "paying" the kid if he didn't get his act together in school. While I didn't realize and notice a pattern 'til the end of the school year and he tested positive for ADHD, he was about to come up missing on his payments. Or maybe just come up missing altogether.

August 31, 2015

Mommy: Kordelle what is this?!

Kordelle: The third letter of the alphabet.

Mommy: What is it doing on your homework?!

Kordelle: Maybeeeeee the first and second letters of the alphabet were busy?

I put my face in my palm and shook my head at my kid.

September 01, 2015
#LunchboxChronicles

Kid: here you go mommy

Mommy: what's this?

Kid: the plastic bag you gave me for lunch today

Mommy: [Insert confused annoyed face HERE]

Mommy: you bring THIS home?! wait, kid where's the actual lunchbox from yesterday?

Kid: I blame the republicans. They take everything. (shakes his head and walks away)

[Insert extra confused annoyed face HERE]

They don't make things like they used to. House, cars, kids. Kids these days don't seem to be phased by anything. You punish them and they shrug it off like it's no big deal. As a kid if you told me that I couldn't go out to play, it was like a death sentence.

I specifically remember when having the cool themed plastic lunch box was "a thing." It was a thing, right? At the beginning of the school year we would try to show up with the coolest box. And kids were ruthless, if you didn't have the cool themed lunch box, you would have been teased and made fun of. So here I was thinking I was going to show my mini a thing or two, teach him a lesson: maybe if he got teased by his peers he would learn to keep up with the cooler version of his stuff (don't judge me for putting my mini in the line of fire, it was for his own good). Nothing for him to come home, lesson-unlearnt. See, his peers could care less about cool lunch boxes. They had other things to be worried about. Like, ridiculous Minecraft YouTube videos. HOW IN THEE ENTIRE WORLD is it entertaining to watch a video of other people playing video games?! I just don't understand kids these days! The one trait that is congruent with the youth of today and the youth of yesterday is that kids are still ruthless. THAT part has stayed consistent. But the stuff they are ruthless about escapes me. #shrugs

September 04, 2015
We moved about 45min from my son's school. But it's one of the best so I keep him there. Each evening I prepare spiritual lessons for my son & I. Then on our long commute every morning we listen to an audio bible app

& discuss the teachings of how they apply to our lives today & ways to be better Christians. I'm far from perfect, & still love my trap music after he gets out the whip lol. But we find the time to assess our imperfections. If you want something bad enough, you'll grow through enough things to figure it out.

September 18, 2015

When your child gets in trouble at school, the teacher usually calls at the end of the day. So when the school's # shows up DURING the day, you freak out thinking he's about to die.

(Voicemail from the kid)

Kid: so. Mommy. Hi. (Long pause) I love you. & uhhhh (pause) so we got these grades in reading right. & I was just calling to let you know that I got a bad grade. BUT I DID THE WORK. I just forgot to turn it in. & I uhhhhh was calling nowwwwwww sooooo you could process it anddddd let it simmer beforeeeeeeee I see you this afternoon. And I uhhhh love you and hope you have a great day. Oh. & (all in one breath) ithinkmy-lunchboxgotthrownawayonaccidentitwasntmyfaultloveyoubye.

(Dial Tone)

Soooooo... He calls to pre-empt me? Smh ughhhhhhhhhhhh thank GOD it's Friday!

October 19, 2015

& now it's time for another installment of #LunchBoxChronicles

Kid's dad: yeaaaa I couldn't pack him a lunch because...Well go 'head tell her.

Me: tell me what?

Kid: I don't know where my lunchbox is

Me: whutchu mean? Kidddddd I JUST replaced that lunchbox!

Kid: it could be at karate...Or the bus...Or at grandmas.

[Insert semi pregnant pause HERE]

Or at school. I... Just don't know mom I'm sorry.

Me: guess you won't be eating today.

Kid: I can still eat, I think Grandma put money in my lunch account

Me: kid... You got one chance to tell me why I shouldn't spank you

Kid: ok. Well. For starters. And you know. So in my defense...Ok I got nothing. MOM IM TRYING TO BE A GENIUS IM TOO BUSY REMEMBERING ALL THE SMART STUFF I FORGET BASIC STUFF LIKE A LUNCHBOX IM SORRY PLEASE DONT SPANK ME I HAVE STRAIGHT A's NOW.

Mom: you're cleaning all the toilets when we get home

Kid: wait. I take it back. No no spank me spank me!

I forgot my little genius is a germaphobe! Mommy wins!

Did I mention that I don't know what I'm doing? I think I mentioned that early on in this book. I have no clue. I tap into my memory bank of things my mom used to do, or stories that my abuela told me, try to emulate and get through this thing called life without crashing and burning too bad.

At the beginning of each new year, I usually stop to re-evaluate life. This includes my parenting skills. And even while I re-read these posts to compile in our memoirs of love and adventure, it dawned on me...

...my son is extremely manipulative. I can't say I blame him or I even fault him because he definitely gets it honestly. As I continued to evaluate his antics, I realized that they weren't a behavior trait. They were character flaws. Him being manipulative will never change.

While it is my job to instill in him values, traditions, and morals—to fill him up with positivity and greatness—he didn't come to me empty. The day he was born, who and how he would be were already ingrained within him. While we do pick up mannerisms along the way, that wasn't one of them; he was born a jerk. I'm sure some over-the-top parent is going to take offense to this, but I don't particularly care that much. People are people no matter the age. I mean, I don't love him any less. I'm just calling a spade a spade.

Instead of harping on him 'til he is eighteen about how to be less of a manipulative prick, I chose to confront it head on. It's kinda' cute while he's young, but by the time he becomes a teenager, I'll be over it. So I decided to help him hone his trait in a positive direction. I directly addressed it with him. Broke down the word manipulation, had him look it up in the dictionary, and explained to him that while he may not know what he was doing, I had peeped game and wasn't feeling it at all.

Of course he looked confused. I told him that as he got older this would make more sense. I told him he needed to use it towards things that are righteous and good. Influence people to do what you want in a positive manner that was pleasing to God, and seek avenues to help others help themselves. It didn't make sense then, but I had to start molding his thought process before he realizes the power in his trait and uses it for bad. I wish the mothers of our modern-day politicians had done that with their kids thirty-five years ago or so.

October 21, 2015

I've developed patience. Discernment. Empathy. Humility. Compassion. Responsibility. A wine habit...

My son is the best thing that ever happened to me. Legit would've been lost without this lunchbox-losing 'lil dude. Thanks Kid for making me grow up.

I hope my sharing will help someone. Lord knows I wish I would've had a "me" back then. My son literally saved my life. Working so hard to provide for him is my thank you, whether it is to him or to God; I just know I owe somebody a thank you—my silent appreciation for another chance.

When I was younger, I had tons of gastrointestinal problems. Long story short (skipping all of the sappy details) after a few experimental drugs and procedures, I was told that I was infertile. I met my son's father at a time in my life when I was full blown out of control. My parents did an awesome job raising me, but I had been almost too sheltered. I got a taste of freedom and lost my mind. I got my own apartment during freshman year of college and started partying heavy, drinking heavy, even started experimenting with drugs. And while I truly was on a path of destruction, I was working two jobs with a salary more than some of my friends' parents. I was a full-time student on the Dean's list, and I was paying for school [by that time] out of pocket. Who was gonna' check me huh? That answer was simple: God.

Sometimes God calms the storm. Other times, God lets the storm rage to calm us. I met my son's father at a house party I had thrown one winter. Although I was already dating someone else, we became inseparable after that night. We fussed and argued like any couple, but we loved so hard. Until recently, I had never met anyone who loved me as much and as unconditionally as he did.

You ever meet someone that was so good *to* you but so bad *for* you? That was us. Unintentionally, he enabled me to do and be everything I ever wanted—both good and bad. He supported all of my dreams, desires, and habits. The level of spoiled-ness that I've reached because of him was never undone and we spiraled out of control to dangerous levels together. Then came my twenty-first birthday.

We got into a huge fight that night after having unprotected sex, and didn't speak for a while, a VERY long while after, even though we lived together. Never met someone who could hold a grudge? Hi my name is Tai; nice to meet you.

Over the next few months, I started to gain weight. I was never a slim girl so it wasn't *that* big of a deal, but after about twenty-one pounds in a few months, it became noticeable. I signed up for a three-year gym membership to Bally's. I worked out twice a day for two weeks… and gained another pound. I wasn't doing anything but cardio, so it wasn't muscle weight. I was studying to take the Medical College Admission Test (MCATs) and we had just finished discussing thyroid disorders. "That's it! My thyroid is broken!" To the doctor I went.

After checking in, the front desk chick told me that I had missed my women's wellness visit for that year and asked if I wanted to get that taken care of as well. I told her sure. The doctor told me that she was going to do the pap smear first.

While she was down there fiddling around, she exclaimed hesitantly, "Oh, well I'm going to cancel your thyroid test and referral."

I asked why.

She said, "Because your cervix is flipped."

My response: "Ok… unflip it." The gently aged Indian doctor said, "No you don't get it. Your cervix flips when you're pregnant."

I flipped out. "I can't be pregnant. That requires penis, and I haven't had sex in months!" (Remember that grudge I had mentioned? Yep, still had it.)

"I can't even have children. See that's why it's called practicing medicine. Y'all are so simple; you don't know what you're talking about, just making educated assumptions."

Mid spazz-out, the doctor moved over to the hole in the wall where I had placed my urine sample inside of the metal turnstile. Unbeknownst to me, she had dipped a pregnancy test in the sample, and as sure as the sky is blue, that thang read, "PREGNANT."

"Who's the simple one now?" she asked. "I'll see you in two weeks for your pre-natal check-up." She stepped out of the room and left me with my circle of thoughts.

"I can't have a baby.

I still AM a baby."

I cut out the partying. The drinking. The drugs. I got serious about college. While I ended up dropping out three times, changed my major eight times, took six and a half years to finish and amassed more than a semester's worth of tuition in parking tickets, I finally graduated… with TWO degrees. It wasn't just me anymore. My path of destruction was detoured with a construction created by God. And yea, I stray. But my son… ahhh that guy keeps me grounded. I was scared out of my mind like, "I can't have a kid! I'm too irresponsible for a kid! I don't make enough money! How am I going to feed him?"

All of that was true, but if you haven't figured it out or are in the same position *now* that I was in *then,* and want to fast forward to the end of the story, baby 'I'mma let you know: everything will be alright. I've read the conclusion and *The End* ends just fine.

November 15, 2015
Being forced to listen to why Kordelle broke up with his last girlfriend,
stayed single for a week, then started dating an older girl because she was
smarter. While I applaud the upgrade, I'm still not okay with any of this
puppy love.

November 16, 2015 7:03AM
I act a fool. A complete fool. & this kid just lets me, pays me no mind.

November 16, 2015 7:09AM
(It started bc the kid tried to stop me from stealing a muffin out of his
lunchbox...)
Otw to his school I turned the music down and screamed-yelled at him at
the top of my lungs for no reason. He opened one eye, looked at me, then
went back to dozing off.
I'm appalled like "he's immune to my crazy???? gotta kick it up a
notch!"
So I wait til he's almost in a good deep sleep then SLAM ON BRAKES!
(Made sure no one was behind us) the seatbelt cut off his air for a quick
second.
Kid: (he looks over choking and yells) what is wrong with you?! You're
crazy!!"
Mommy: (now content) & don't you ever forget it!

November 17, 2015
#LunchboxChronicles (yep... two in one week)

Kid: mommy I thought you said you were going to make me breakfast this
school year?

Mommy: I was until your school started offering free breakfast to all kids. & it aint een free for real bc my taxes pay for that. So let my taxes feed you & be happy.

Kid: but... Your taxes don't buy good food. Rachel Maddow says your taxes buy stuff with preservatives & GMOs. You must want me to get sick & die off GMOs.

(Crickets...Crickets)

Mommy: kid you're not a morning person you don't een get up early enough to eat breakfast if I were to cook it.

Kid: you could fix it to-go

Mommy: to-go? Like in a to-go box? YOU DONT EVEN KEEP UP WITH YOUR LUNCH BOX NOW YOU WANT A BREAKFAST BOX!!?...

(Long pause)

Kid: GMOs. If I die from GMOs, you're going to be lonely. And bored. SUPER bored.

November 26, 2015 11:45PM- Inner Harbor, MD

I debated whether I should post this or not. I don't want attention; you post selfies for stuff like that. I want to shine attention on a huge problem in my city. We all just finished stuffing ourselves to capacity laughing and joking with family, making plates to take home and overeat for the rest of the week... While thousands starve. I saw how much leftovers we had and how blessed we are... Packed up the truck and took some friends to the streets of Baltimore to feed the homeless.

Met Jerry, Mike, and several others who are cold and forgotten. This week I know you have leftovers... Instead of stashing them for yourself... Maybe think of sharing them with your brothers and sisters, be His vessel. Be the change you want to see in the world. -Gandhi. #Agape

I usually fuss with myself about whether to share what I've dubbed to be glory stories or not; the ones that people usually glamorize when they are looking for attention and gold stars? In a world so full of people that brag to get accolades and pats on the back, all I want is to inspire and encourage other people to think about more than just themselves. I don't want to receive my rewards from the world. I think I have misinterpreted Matthew 6:2 (lol) thus I am always hesitant to share. If I receive nothing back, whether from the world or from God, it's ok. I received my reward in being a blessing.

We are so gluttonous as a people. We hoard money, clothes, shoes, food, and then we complain when we find ourselves without and lacking. If we could only consistently live beneath our means we would have more than enough resources to help everyone: the haves AND the have nots. Baltimore is so overrun with homelessness and stricken with drugs and poverty. Our winters are nothing to play with.

While I am not always one to stop and give to every homeless person, my family had food for days, for weeks even.

As we drove our fat full bellies past homeless people every day, I was uneasy with my cup running over that night knowing we didn't need it.

December 9, 2015
#LunchboxChronicles

(The Kid goes to a school TOTALLY out of our district. & although I fell madly in love w/ our house... Not in love with the schools. So I drive 45min every morning M-F to make sure he has a great education.)

Kid: sooooo... My teacher was pressing me out about why I had been late to school the last few days
Mom: ...and?
Kid: ... I told the truth.
Mom: KID! What you do that for kid?! Now I have to go do damage control
Kid: well what was I supposed to do?!
Mom: you could've plead the fifth!!!
Kid: ...what's that?

(As we walk through the mall later that day buying new school shoes bc the kid apparently has a fashion sense now & hates the Stacy Adams I just bought him, I explain his Constitutional Rights & Amendments as a US Citizen)

Kid: (we walk by a children's boutique store) Hey my girlfriend has a lunchbox just like that one [kid points to some shiny glittery girly looking thing with bows]

Mom: your WHAT? Your girlfriend?! We talked about this, focus on books. Girls are stupid & they lie! What does she look like? Is she smart is she a Democrat?!
Kid: (looks at me and smiles) I plead the fifth.

I swear I sound like my mom, but the only thing that popped in my head for me to tell my son was, "You have all of the time in the world to be an adult, and such a short amount of time to be a kid. Baby, just enjoy being a kid. Dating will come, girlfriends will come. Just focus on school kid." I'm an adult now and how quickly we forget—because my parents had the same conversation with me about boys several times, and it never sank in. I didn't start this young but, times change. Kids are made from a different cloth than we were. Which is why I often question when are we supposed to have "the talk" with kids nowadays?! I've tried a few times and have been very unsuccessful. Gotta ask YouTube; everything is on YouTube!

December 10, 2015
Kid: "mommyyyyyyyy shushhhhh...CNN is on. Smh I don't like any of these presidential candidates."
Mommy: DTFL

The Kid is a staunch democrat. He gets so worked up over politics I have to make him go watch cartoons. I have no idea where he picked it up, but I constantly struggle with him enjoying his childhood, "No CNN Kordelle. Go watch the Cartoon Network."

#LUNCHBOXCHRONICLES

December 22, 2015
#LunchboxChronicles

I talk about "our Christmas" every year & I'm proud about the tradition we've created. I don't knock anyone else's holiday approach... But I stopped subscribing to the holiday capitalism long ago. We live in a generation flooded by laziness. Yep I said it. Used to instant gratification & handouts; getting blessed with everything their parents never had has crippled my generation.

Kordelle gets three things for Christmas: 1 thing he wants, 1 thing he needs, 1 thing I would like for him to have. We cook breakfast together, play a bit, then spend the rest of the day helping others. I stopped understanding why we flood our children w/ presents... It's not their b-days lol its, "Jesus's"... So...We give Him presents in great abundance in acts of service & love.

I will never infringe upon someone my thoughts & beliefs. But maybe think of taking a step back & see the longitudinal negative effects our holiday actions have on our community: spending more than we have overextending our finances, gluttony, hoarding, & collecting things we don't truly NEED bc if we did...We wouldn't have waited til now to get it.

When I speak to my millennials & they lack drive, hard work ethics, knowing how to live beneath their means or to go without; running back home or expecting parents to continually bail them out of life situations...
I am driven to further attempt to protect my son from ME: crippling & enabling him via love & presents.

Just my two cents that no one asked for but I donated anyways.
Happy Holidays #thereasonfortheseason #steppingoffmysoapbox
PS: he's TOTALLY getting a new lunchbox for Christmas

This tradition started a few years ago. I was sitting at the kitchen table and Kordelle asked me a question. Though serious in his inquiry, it came out a bit rude, "Mommy, have you started on my Christmas list yet?"

I'mma pause there. I was having a really really bad day at this time, back when he was three or four. We had just moved into a new apartment. It was freezing cold as we rushed in for the night. Kordelle bombarded me with questions about Christmas, "Did you give Santa our new address? Do we have a chimney? We don't have a chimney; how is he going to get our presents to us?"

My answer to all of his queries was that "Everything is going to be alright Kordelle." But his last revelation pushed me over the edge as I was cold and already having a bad day, "I've got it! We can leave the front door open so he can come in, and the back door open with cookies next to it so he can get out!" I snapped and blurted out, "Kordelle there is no Santa Clause. I AM SANTA CLAUSE!" He looked at me with his bright eyes and said, "You take that back."

"No. Hell no! I bust my butt to take care of you and provide for you, and buy you presents. I'll be darn if I allow some mystical morbidly obese man to take the credit for my sacrifices!" Smh… I wouldn't recommend telling them that early; let me just say that.

I digress. Several years later and the kid knows the routine. After I told him that I hadn't started on his Christmas list, he then asked in the sweetest voice, "Are you waiting for an invitation?" I shrugged off his out of place, but innocent, comment. I was finishing up grad school and my paper was due in sixteen minutes.

Next thing I knew, I heard the kid clear his throat from behind my laptop. "Ahem." I kept typing. He cleared his throat louder this time, "AHEM." I peeked over the top of my laptop as my son gave me a formal presentation, "I, Kordelle Hall, cordially invite you, Mommy Hall, to myyyyyy Christmas List. Everything I would like can be found at Target."

I paused and just blinked. Didn't know whether to discipline him for his curtness, be impressed by his well-put-together presentation, or to just keep typing. I was just overwhelmed with a tinge of anger and annoyance. I wasn't mad at my son's directness. The reality of what Christmas had become and how we had perverted it over the decades no longer sat right with me.

I asked aloud, "Wait, why am I buying YOU presents anyways? It's not even your birthday. It's Jesus's birthday!" My son thought about my question and said, "Well, because that's a tradition that everyone always does." I told him, "Well maybe we need to start a new tradition."

He said, "Ok. What kind of presents does Jesus want?"

I had never thought about it lol. "I guess Jesus wants peace. And love." My son got excited and said, "No problem, where can we buy love at?"

Laughing, I told him that if he knew the answer to that, we could capitalize on it and get rich quick. "But until we do, we have to give love the old-fashioned way. By doing and caring for others." And ever since then, I decided that we were going to have our own Christmas morals, traditions, values, and ideals. We've practiced them ever since. Instead of the over the top unnecessary abundance of gifts that children usually don't need, Kordelle gets three: (1) one thing he wants, (2) one thing he needs, (3) and one thing that I would like him to have. I noticed a while ago, even within my own life journey: we rarely appreciate the things we have in our lives if we didn't earn them. Relationships, cars, food, money; etc. We blow through and disrespect things and people we didn't have to work for. Kids grow up not appreciating much of anything—well, you never required them to. When we spend decades blessing children with gifts they never earn, it becomes quite cumbersome to switch that mindset and expect them to do the opposite. Or even worse, they are shy away from the hardwork, and still expect the world. All due to American capitalistic traditions. Way to go [insert sarcastic high-five HERE]!I usually send him on scavenger hunts to find his presents. I use a combination of whatever they are currently teaching him in school with my educational twist to create the scavenger hunt clues. To find his presents, he has to answer the problems correctly or he'll wind up at a dead end and will have to back track. The clues wind up taking him all around our home, to the car, the street corner light, the side porch and back around again. Eventually he finds all three presents.

Most times one of them involves a trip with the plane tickets pinned to our travel map. All of the states that we've been to have a huge push pin in them. Other times, he receives small, but super thoughtful gifts, like a laptop with a new desk and chair set already put together. Or maybe just a pack of pencils he really needs. Our holidays have become practical, loving, and focused around giving back to others more than ourselves.

December 28, 2015

Hair curled. Bags packed. Wine in suitcase. Yep I'm ready! #IndianaBound

December 28, 2015

Praise break with people we don't know in the parking lot of the gas station that loved my playlist & our singing at the top of our lungs. "God don't move my mountain, but give me the strength to climb!" They said we made their day! #JustHisvessels!

December 29, 2015
Kid: mommy what's a period?
Mommy: a punctuation at the end of a sentence
Kid: no. Thee OTHER period
Me: (insert deer in headlights HERE)

Poor child. I had been so hormonal the past few days. And I suppose he overheard my conversation of me telling my mom that I was on my period. A few hours later he asked me. And, so I...I told him! I don't remember exactly all that I said, but it was pretty close to the truth. I vaguely remember saying something about if a man's DNA doesn't swim up to have a party with a woman's egg, then her body gets rid of the party juice. And it makes the woman mean and cranky for no reason. He looked so confused. Then, I cut the cute talk and told him the truth. He took a moment to process it, then said "ok."

The next month I was going OFF about something and the kid said, "Mom are you doing that period thing again?" I DIED OF LAUGHTER, and what's even funnier is that I was actually on my period.

December 29, 2015 - Indianapolis, IN
And irrelevant to the fact that there is frozen water coming out of the sky...
Kordelle wants me to teach him how to ride his bike. Please hold while I
make a glove run. Smh THIS experiment should be interesting.

I was trying to spend our last day in Indiana, before heading to Kentucky, in the warm, safe house. Kordelle had other plans. At least he was sticking to the original plans I had agreed to before frozen tear drops started plummeting the earth. I told the kid that I didn't have any gloves. He observantly pointed out that there was a J.C. Penny's across the street.

Reluctantly, we went to make a glove run. We picked out some gloves just as quickly as we had come, and went to stand in line. While in line, my son made a very startling observation. He said, "Mommy, why do the men mannequins have heads, but the women mannequins don't?"

It is crazy how desensitized we become over time to things that actually matter. What's even crazier is what we allow to persist as a part of our normalcy. I had to break down so many grown up life lessons to a child that I was still digesting myself. I tried to dumb down this one in layman's terms that I hoped he could ingest. I struggled to explain marketing, sexism, and the objectification of women in American culture. While I am not a feminist, I couldn't help but become disgusted by the entire department store which was covered in beheaded female mannequins. Before we left, I told my mini to ask for the manager and pose his question to her. She looked bewildered and blinked a few times as if that was the first time she had even noticed it herself. I shook my head and we left to go learn how to ride his Christmas present in the snow.

December 30, 2015
#LunchboxChronicles

Kid: Dragon? Can I have a dragon?
Mom: I don't know. Can you?
Kid: (deep sigh) May I have a dragon?
Mom: You can't keep up with your lunchbox how are you going to keep up with a...No
Kid: Pet pig?
Mom: No

Kid: Venus flytrap?
Mom: Those are real?! No
Kid: Flying squirrels? A hedgehog? a chinchilla?
Mom: No, no, & TF?
Kid: A baby brother?
Mom: What kind of dragon you want?

January 02, 2016 - Louisville, KY
I have found that Dixie Disgust I've been hearing about. In the form of 380lbs + curls, pearls, & a snarled peach lip. Hayyyy boo I see you! I walked over & told her I hope you have an amazing day before leaving (insert red hair flip HERE)

By the time we had made it to Kentucky, I had been warned enough times by my friends and family not to sass any cops while I was there (yep, I need those kinds of pep talks smh). But for the most part, Kentucky was chill! Had no issues or concerns. Didn't even notice anything as being out of the ordinary until I went to go donate blood. And BOOM there it was. But what can I say? I was a redhead walking contradiction covered in tattoos and piercings with a fondness for flexing vintage SAT words for no reason. #killemwithkindness

January 30, 2016
#LunchboxChronicles

Unpacking the kid's lunchbox & I find some girls telephone # in it. At the same time a Viagra commercial was on. Kinda went off the deep end and tried to talk to him about sex. He shut me down so quick.

Mom: Kid, what do you know about sex?

Kid: Mom... I don't want to learn anything new today

Mom: tf? Wait... So you don't know what sex is? (Long pause) OR DO YOU NOT WANT TO TALK TO ME ABOUT IT?!

Kid: I don't want to talk to you about sex

Mom: So you lied to me a second ago...WITH A STRAIGHT FACE?!

Kid: Not exactly

Mom: So exactly what're you saying then because I'm confused? You don't know what sex is OR you don't want to talk to me about sex?!

Kid: ...both! (Kid sticks fingers in his ears and moonwalks away)

...10min later...

Kid: Hey where's Bill Cosby?

Mom: Probably in jail...BECAUSE OF SEX you ready to talk about it yet?!

Kid: I know not of that of which you speaketh

Still haven't quite figured out that sex talk thing yet lol. I will get it one of these days. I told him that he would have to talk to me about it eventually. Maybe he's not comfortable talking to *me* about it. I suggested that he talk to my boyfriend, or his dad, or maybe my dad. He (get this) said he would like to reschedule talking to me about it until the next week. Next week?! A whole week is going to make a difference?! He said it would. Told me that he would have time to prepare himself. Whatever that means. UPDATE: "next week" still hasn't come as of yet.

January 31, 2016
My house smells like food & love

February 02, 2016
#LunchboxChronicles

Not even a funny one. Just draining.

Mom: (last night as we're getting out of the truck) Grab your book bag &
the rest of your stuff on the way in the house
Kid: So... I don't have "stuffs"
Mom: Kid... Where's your book bag?
Kid: I left it in Ms. Tiffany's trunk when she picked me up today
Mom: ughhhh just grab your lunchbox then
Kid: I left that too

Woke up dumb early to drive nineteen minutes out of the way on top of our forty-two minute commute to go on a book bag retrieval mission so he could turn his homework in on time.

March 10, 2016
Can't go home. Cops are there waiting for me. I'm officially a fugitive. Won't give the rental car back bc I still need it/Insurance companies said they had updated the reservation but CLEARLY someone didn't. I have places to go NO YOU Can't HAVE THE WHIP YET TIL I GET A NEW ONE. I just made all of yall my accomplices. #igodownyougodown #bringingallofFBwithme #copperswontgetme #kissmybumper #justkissit

We were in a really bad car accident on February 12. My brand new truck of less than six months was totaled. Some guy (that's an upgrade to what I had been calling him) stopped too short in the rain in morning traffic. He plowed into the back of us, and pushed me into a utility van in front of us. We were the only ones who had to go to the hospital. Our vehicle was the only one that had to be towed. Smh, it was a rough day to say the least.

Fast forward a few weeks or so; the insurance companies were fighting over which ones was going to pay for my rental car. Although the guy had insurance, he didn't have enough. Thus his insurance company dropped any assistance and coverage they were extending to me. This included the rental. My insurance company argued that they weren't required to pay for the rental. It was just an all-around mess.

Meanwhile, the bill for the rental car was steadily climbing! Enterprise called and threatened me to pay, they even texted me! Companies text now?! I refused to give them the car back. They said they were sending the cops to my house. I didn't believe them. So when I got home and there were three Baltimore City police cars in front of my home, I figuratively shat two bricks, drove around the block, parked down the street, and the kid and I slid into the house through the back door.

I instructed him to not make any sudden movements, stay away from the windows, and don't turn on any lights. Lol only for me to find out a few minutes later that the cops were there for my neighbors across the street who were running a prostitution and drug ring out of their connected garage. The insurance companies figured out the rental car situation the next day. But I was a full-blown fugitive for like a half a day.

My next-door neighbor was too cool. I only had...have, one and I adore her. She knows everything about everything there is to know. She had been there forever and a day and has seen a lot. She took a strong liking to Kordelle and I and was super impressed once she heard my story of how and what God has brought us through. Not even to mention the story about the house.

How could I forget the story about the house?! I'll short version it for you. I had lived in Baltimore before. The beginning of this book starts out with me explaining that I was moving out of my parent's home for the last time and into my own apartment in Hyattsville, Maryland. But what about before then? Everyone has a "before then" and mine was definitely note-worthy.

I had separated from my son's father years prior. Our lives had spiraled out of control except I changed, and he didn't. He has since, and we co-parent quite cohesively actually. But then? Nope, we were at emotional war. And the only thing I could afford at the time, not to mention it was minutes driving distance from my then job at Best Buy Corporate in Jessup, MD, was a super hood complex in Baltimore called Cherry Hill.

When I told my friends that I had moved into Cherry Hill, they keeled over in laughter explaining that most people spend their entire lives trying to get out of Cherry Hill, but my dumb ass had moved in. #shrugs

While finishing up undergrad, I took up a bartending job at a bar not too far from where I lived in my West Baltimore apartment-style townhome. The owner's husband started to hate on me which was the beginning of my downward spiral before God sent a come-up. Side note: I need to also mention my father and I didn't have the best relationship at the time, and I had asked for God to help me fix my relationship with my family. This was before the hero blow up. It wasn't bad, just… estranged. Maybe it was bad #moreshrugs I just knew I loved them and wished we were better. Whether it was my fault or theirs, I just wanted *us* to be better.

Along with finishing undergrad, I had just started massage school, which was about twelve minutes away from our apartment. I took out loans for eighty-five percent of my vocational attendance, and my dad wrote me monthly checks for the rest, which I paid him back in full four years later. He has always supported my dreams. We had a weird relationship that pushed the spectrum edge of pain and love further than the norm on both sides.

Attending two schools didn't afford too many opportunities for occupational success. I enrolled in a two-week bartending program in Virginia (yep, I'm the epitome of a hustler). I took up this new endeavor after getting fired from a retail gig for rearranging their store front (my way made more sense. The district manager wound up calling and thanking me but 'whatevs'). I started bartending around the way. The bar was a posh hole-in-the-wall that attracted everyone from politicians, electricians, comedians, and drug dealers; just your typical neighborhood watering hole with great food and great music.

Everyone loves the single mom in school story. I wasn't trying to get any kudos, but it just so happened to be my reality. Genuine convo and a smile, along with the single mom story went a long way, and patrons started tipping me more than they were spending in the bar. The owner's husband, a jealous man with bad business ethics, noted how much money was walking out the door, and got in his wife's ear, "We need to fire Tai. Tai is stealing. Tai isn't ringing up drinks. Tai needs to go." After a few months, the owner, a nice shapely woman whose daughter and I had become friends, pulled me up and apologized but informed me they were letting me go, "…I'm sorry this is a partnership and my husband just doesn't trust you."

I rarely beg. But I damn sure did that day. I begged for them not to let me go. I begged her to hear me out. I was living paycheck-to-paycheck as my pride wouldn't allow me to apply for government assistance and my son's father wasn't paying child support. I was literally living off of that job. They canned me anyways, and I lost everything.

I fell behind on rent, was evicted, and threw what I wanted to salvage into storage. I ran out of money to eat and lived out of my car struggling to finish school and find work. I carried on this way until I ran out of the last bit of money and resources I had to feed my son.

I humbled myself and asked my parents if I could move back in. They had no idea what all had transpired, but knew it had to be bad for me to ask. My dad didn't want me to come back. Not because he didn't love me. But because I mean… they had grown used to me not being there. Not to mention my dad and I already struggled to co-exist in long spans of time. It was a power struggle before I was eighteen. It damn sure was about to be one now that I was older. Additionally, when I left, it was just me. Now returning? I had a plus one.

I finished schools, saved up money while paying them rent and reducing some debt, moved out into our own apartment again (after the Hero blow up), started my first business, and bought a house.

The day I move into my beautiful Historic Victorian I ran into my only real neighbor as my home is a corner lot. We get to rappin' and she says, "It's so sad what happened to the previous owners."

I halted uber fast like, "Pause! Did somebody die up in this house?! Because I checked the public records and it ain't say nothing about nobody dying up in here!"

"No, girl ain't nobody die. They were club owners," she said.

"Oh. They lost all their money by pouring it into the club?" I asked.

"Yep. Basically," she said, trying to recall the details. "It was in a racist neighborhood and the rednecks over there kept calling the cops on them."

"Tuuh, I know how that can be. I used to bartend at this bar over in Pigtown. They were as racist as they come. And the guys that used to come bang with us up at the bar weren't the most upstanding citizens you know. D-boys are only going to rock with you but for so long with cops always poppin' up on them," I told her.

"And it was such a cute little club. Dernit I wish I could remember the name of it. Over there off Washington Boulevard," my neighbor said.

My fingers went numb—not from holding the boxes I was going to take inside of my brand-new home—but from piecing together the facts of what she had just said. Washington Boulevard was in Pigtown. And though it's been sometime since I had lived in Baltimore, it hadn't changed but so much. There weren't too many establishments that had come through Pigtown.

"What was the name of this club?" I asked her nervously.

She said, "It was called Club something…Club…Club…Cl.

"Club Reality?!" I finished her sentence for her.

"That's it there you go! Club Reality!"

I dropped the boxes that I was holding and started to cry in disbelief. In astonishment. In anger. In ironic happiness, "Are you telling me that the people that owned Club Reality used to own this house?!"

"Yep!"

I had looked for a house for over two years. I had toured over fifty houses. Had a contract on six…seven including this one. They all fell through except for *this* house. And when it came to this house, I had *thee* most problems from start to finish. However, God handled every issue that arose with grace and swiftness.

I told my new neighbor what had happened. I explained how they ruined my life. She listened and said, "Girl won't He do it! Will make your enemies your foot stool! Glad to have you. I wasn't the biggest fan of them anyways!"

#LUNCHBOXCHRONICLES

Capítulo Siete

#Riots
{voces de la ignorada}

Moving to Baltimore has taught me several lessons. One of the biggest is that we over coddle our children in suburban communities, crippling them of their ability to survive, denying them proper development of cognitive life thinking skills, and enable them further than they need. It's just like a garden that's fussed over too much and the crops wither and die.

May 24, 2016
#LunchBoxChronicles

Mom: Where's your lunchbox Kid?
Kid: Ummm I don't know
Mom: Who shot Tupac?
Kid: What?
Mom: Where's Biggie?
Kid: Huh?
Mom: (face to palm) I've failed you. Look yo, you gotta know the answer to ONE of these questions!!!
Kid: I uhhh (scratches head) guess I'll go look for Biggie

As I kept skimming through my Facebook posts, I noticed that the dates were getting spaced out. The stories started to get few and far between. Sigh…Kordelle was growing up. I wouldn't go as far as to say he was getting more responsible as he didn't stop losing stuff altogether. School ended for the year, and I started sending him with paper bag lunches to summer camp.

The quality and temperature of our conversations changed over the summer as I opted to take Kordelle out of the Prince George's County Public School System and placed him into a Baltimore City Charter school. The commute had started to consume us, not to mention the school's inability to deal with my son's uncharted disability.

I just didn't want my baby to be labeled. I wanted to receive help, but not to be treated like an outcast as most PG County Public Schools tended to do when a child was "different." Towards the end of the school year, we all suffered. He suffered. My parents suffered going back and forth to the school to give him last minute things that he left, or aiding us in finishing projects on a Sunday afternoon because Kordelle didn't remember them until the day before, and I was running around playing the business version of Carmen Sandiego with massage clients. I suffered. His grades suffered.

His teachers had some "system" in what they did and they didn't allow the children to do or run back home. This was their attempt to instill in them adult responsibilities; mind you, many adults still struggle with these types of expectations. Even if I am being sensitive to the fact that kids have to learn one way or another, these policies were still counterproductive, because the "life lessons" actually hindered students' social, educational, and mental growth. They were not sensitive to a kid's forgetfulness, even if the child had a medical condition.

We had sat down as a group and discussed that my son had ADHD. I mean let's think about this: here it is the end of the third quarter and you all have been repeating the same routine since the first quarter and my son was still struggling to remember the basics: his agenda book, his homework that was ALREADY COMPLETED, his pencil box. We were a good eight months into the school year and he was still missing the routine, something was wrong here!

In a nutshell, their responses were: "I have over 300 children to teach. I don't have time to run behind any of them."

My response? "Yea, but you only have one child that is now failing. Excuse my directness but that is not a reflection of the child. That is a reflection of YOU."

Of course that didn't go over well. But I had no room for sympathy especially after the standardized test scores came back in and my son had scored off the charts. The test scores average from 300 to 999, with the low end being on the autism and retardation spectrum and the high end being above grade level expectations. Kordelle scored 1044. But had a GPA of 1.8 with his only A being in gym.

He would leave his agenda book in his first class. By the time he got to his third class, he realized he had left it and asked for permission to go back to get it. They told him "no," and gave him a zero for whatever work he did not complete or turn in. The teachers gave him a sheet of paper to write down his homework questions for the next day. Between the end of school, after care, and home, that sheet of paper was lost. My son was so embarrassed that he lost the paper, he did not speak up to mention it, no matter how much I stressed the importance of communication and rushed to complete all of the night's homework the next morning before first period started.

I get it. My son was irresponsible, forgetful, clumsy…and struggling. With all of these labels he started to regress in school but continually tested off of the charts. Every school we attended asked me if I would allow them to skip him because of his high-test scores. We tried it once. Socially, my little one needed to stay where he was.

I begged for the school system to help us but to no avail. We struggled as a family 'til the end of the school year. With a retiring principal that seemed to care less about her job and more about her retirement, and a teacher that seemed like she needed a man and some constant dick in her life to take the stick out of her ass before coming to school each morning, I wrote out a supplementary curriculum over the summer and filled in the gaps that my baby missed from a failing public school system that no longer serviced us.

I applied to all forty-four charter schools in Baltimore before the end of that school year, and was elated to find out we had been accepted into three. We enrolled at an academy over East for the following school year, and spent the summer fixing his grades, his routines, and his self-esteem as that last semester left my son feeling inept.

Before the start of the next year, I did some research. I looked up the yellow school bus routes as well as the new school's after care program. There were no school busses. Welcome to Baltimore. The kids here don't have yellow school buses to charter them to and fro. That was one of my first eye-opening realizations that forever changed how I raised Kordelle. The other was that I couldn't afford the new school's after care costs. His new school was in a very affluent neighborhood with very affluent pricing. Baltimore realized years ago the disparity of children based upon the socioeconomic housing; which is pretty consistent with most of Maryland: live in the better neighborhoods, your children attended the better schools.

But should that be the case? Should a child's education suffer because of where his family can afford to live? Similar to most major cities in America, a lottery system was created, allowing families to enter into random drawings for their children to attend schools of which they would normally be locked out. And while most of the other costs were absorbed, I still made too much on paper to afford his aftercare.

That was until I got fired from my fulltime massage job. When people asked me what happened, I give several answers—depending on how I'm feeling that day—but they're all accurate. Sometimes I say it was divine intervention as I never would have left, but by staying, I later found out was blocking other people's blessings. Other times, I say I had outgrown the place. But the real answer? My mouth.

I have been fired from every job I have ever worked. Every position, every career, every form of employment… I've been fired. I have always struggled with being told what to do. For a split second that hot July afternoon, I walked out of my new GM's office consumed by an, *Oh shit what are you going to do?* moment. For about all of five minutes. Then this calm overcame me. God touched me, spoke into me, and told me I was going to be just fine.

That entire revelation can also be reserved for another book. Just know I no longer had full time employment. The problem that it caused: I was now in struggle-survival mode. I was in "by any means necessary mode." And while I am super awesome and amazing and creative and fantastic, I lack execution and timeliness.

While I was newly broke—on paper and almost in real life—I didn't fill out the paperwork in time to qualify for the free or reduced aftercare. I only had a small frame of time left to submit the paperwork—only a few days if I am not mistaken, from the time I was fired 'til the documents were due. And I missed it. Organizing how the mortgage was getting paid and where food was coming from kind of trumped transportation issues at that exact moment.

The beginning of the school year was fast approaching and I had to figure out what to do with The Kid. I had created my own massage company, Taime Out Massage Studios, about four years prior, but had been dragging my feet with chasing my dreams. It's really hard to pursue your dreams while you're still dedicatedly working for someone else who already did.

But now in struggle-survival mode, I poured myself relentlessly into my passion. Prior to being fired, I opened my first massage practice inside of an already existing sports medical suite in White Oak Silver Spring, MD. With the work schedule I had created, along with balancing traffic, and private in-home clients, there was absolutely no way I would be able to pick Kordelle up from school each day.

School at his academy let out at 2:45 p.m. Monday through Friday. For me to get there on time, I would have to leave work no later than 2 p.m.. Scoop him up, drive home, drop him off in city traffic by 3:50 p.m., and then try to head back to the office in rush hour traffic. The office closed at 5 p.m. as the elevators to the building shut off by 6 p.m. I didn't have an elevator key yet to go down and retrieve clients. It wouldn't make sense. It just wasn't feasible for me to accomplish.

We weren't native Baltimoreans; we were PG County-ers, so I had no friends or family to lean on and ask to pick him up each day. I couldn't leave work. I couldn't afford the aftercare program fees, and I had missed the deadline to receive reduced or free care. There was only one choice: we had to grow up. Both of us. We had to become Baltimoreans.

Baltimore is an entirely different beast when it comes to civility. It's rough. Baltimore never recovered from the effect the drug epidemic had on the city during the 80s, including the number of residual junkies it created. Sheesh. You look at an older average native and they look like they have been through some thangs. Forty-year-old women look sixty. Fifty-year-old men looked like they been through war-driven hell and back. Yet through it all, there is a strong familial presence in Baltimore City.

Whether broken or not, people here are very family oriented. But think: if the parents during the 80s were strung out on drugs, running the streets, getting high, the kids learned to make due; they raised themselves. The stories I hear NOW from the friends that I've made since living in the city blow my mind. They are book worthy all on their own. What those young kids—now adults—did to survive because of the wave of crack-cocaine, no one should have ever had to endure. But they did. And it changed them. It changed the mentality and the cultural climate of the city that was then passed on to their children; the same children that are growing up with my son.

I had to completely change how I reared my son because of his new atmosphere. If not, I wouldn't just be doing him a disservice, but that naive over-coddling could get him killed. Not to mention the outpour temperature change of racism and power struggle that raptured the city between patrons and police…

That whole "Kordelle where's your lunch box," cute intro of this book was dead. Kordelle had to ride the bus home and there were aspects of life from which I couldn't protect him. While riding the bus really is no big deal, it is life changing when you're coming from a lifestyle where you never have to pay attention.

Think about it: when you were younger, your parents looked out for danger for you. How often would you zone out while your parents were driving? Even now, when I'm with my boyfriend, I occasionally check out and don't completely pay attention to my surroundings because I'm in the presence of someone I trust to look out for the both of us. For a child, that goes without saying. When you would cross the street with your parents, *they* were the ones to let you know when it was safe to cross. When you were out in public, they would remind you, "Don't talk to strangers." When you were at a grocery store, they would point out emanate dangers or hazards: don't touch that, stay away from that, push your money back in your pocket.

That isn't inner city living. Even after the drug epidemic, there is a massive amount of broken single-family homes here where parents have to work. As young as five-years-old, kids are raising themselves, because for whatever the reason, the parents aren't necessarily there. They didn't have an upbringing similar to mine or even one similar to how I was raising my son. They didn't have the same core values instilled in them to know right from wrong, or to even mind it when they did. Aside from God, there was no one checking them.

We moved into a Historic, Victorian four-level single family detached home, with a finished basement, front wrap around porch, a walk out veranda on the fourth floor, and decked out stainless steel appliances in the kitchen in a nice-ish neighborhood in West Baltimore—one of the roughest areas in the city. While MY neighborhood was nice, Baltimore is one of the few places I've ever seen where they have half million-dollar homes on one street, and projects on the other side of the same street. No cute little parks in between to separate the two. Nope. Money and projects on the side road.

I thought back to every #LunchBoxChronicles story highlighting my baby's forgetfulness. How little he paid attention. How often he checked out on the world. I thought back to how bad we struggled as a family his last semester in third grade at Kingsford Elementary in PG County, and it scared the crap out of me.

But we had to grow up somehow, because as a single mom with a boyfriend at the time that was loving, but not really the most helpful, we were completely on our own.

I devised a plan to strengthen his weakness. I bought an all-day metro pass for the train in DC twice a week until the beginning of the school year, and handed Kordelle a pen and a pad. I had my own in tow and we boarded the metro. He said, "Where are we going mommy?"

I told him, "Absolutely nowhere." I explained to him that he would be riding the bus home by himself every day this school year and I needed him to start paying attention to his surroundings. I was honest and blunt and explained that it was for his own survival as he would be among the world. "Unlike mommy, the world doesn't care about your forgetfulness."

Each time we rode the metro, we completed drills in ten minute increments, writing down everything that we saw. I would hold my list up so that he couldn't see what I was writing, and I would jot down everything. When my phone alarm went off after ten minutes, we would compare our lists. The drilling process ensued until his list wound up being longer than mine.

Initially his lists were basic and pretty short: he would point out the trees, the birds, the powerlines; he would take note of the woman who got on the train, the sign on the wall, the color of the seats. But as we progressed with these drills each time, his lists became more descriptive. He even started to notate things that I didn't see: the misspelling of words in the scrolling marquee, the name brand shoes some kid was wearing, the amount of people on the train car in front of us.

I started to feel more at ease. On the way home, we would have discussions. I mean real life discussions of potential what ifs and how to handle bad situations. I told him there may come a time when a kid would want his shoes, and I asked him what should he do? He looked at me funny as the thought had never crossed his mind. He was like, "But you work hard for me to get these shoes mommy," glancing down at his flashing LED light up shoes. I rolled my eyes so fast and said, "Boy if you don't give up them damn shoes! I can get you more shoes. I can't get another you. It's one thing to not be wasteful and blatantly disrespect your things out of inconsideration. It's another thing to release them out of necessity. Ain't nothing on your body worth your life you remember that."

I asked him what to do if he accidentally fell asleep on the bus and missed his stop. He said he would call me. I told him, "No, wrong answer."

As a massage therapist, if I'm in session, I may not have my phone on me. "You gonna have to figure it out." I had gotten him a cell phone and initially showed him how to use it. Before long, he was showing me different features I had yet to discover.

He knew the address to our house and how to use the GPS. (Slight fast-forward) a time did come when he overslept. He missed his stop by three stops. He didn't call, but he texted me. I told him to use the GPS' walking feature to route the directions from where he was to where we lived, and text me when he got home. He sent me a screen shot of his commute. It was an eleven minute walk to the house.

(OK rewind) I changed how I answered his questions: his umbrella was stuck in the holder I kept next to the front door, and he was unable to pull it out. It was pouring down raining and we had to go. He asked if I could help him. As I began to move towards the front door to assist him, I said, "No. What would you do if I wasn't here? Figure it out or go without." He didn't figure it out. I knew what was wrong; one of the prongs were caught on a decorative leaf in the holder and it was a certain way he would have had to move it back and then up to release it. But if I continued to think for my son, when would he ever learn to think for himself? It also presented a learning opportunity on prioritizing and resources: if he had spent all of his time trying to release the umbrella, that would have decreased the amount of time he would have be able to spend at the indoor waterpark where we were going. He learned in that moment what is worth his time and when he can go without things.

The expectations I placed upon him in the house a few weeks before school started to change as well. We wrote out his daily chores and placed them on the side of the fridge. They included collecting all of the trash in the house, making his bed, cleaning his room, raking the leaves in the fall, taking the recycle out each Tuesday night and placing the recycle bin alongside the curb, starting my truck each morning, sweeping and moping the floor, washing the dishes (if there was a single dish in my sink after he had gone to bed that night he was abruptly awakened from his slumber to address the issue); the list also included cleaning all of the bathrooms in the house, vacuuming, cleaning the cat litter box, washing his clothes, and dusting to name a few (I think that's most of them to be honest, but there are a few more floating around on that list somewhere).

We would cook together each night and I showed him how to light the stove. He learned how to cook the basics like eggs, bacon, sausage, and chicken. After this, some days I would tell him to go ahead and start dinner for me if I had a long day. He knew to turn the oven to 350 degrees, lay the chicken breasts on parchment paper and season them on both sides using minimal salt, and to set the timer according to how many pieces of chicken we were cooking.

There were days when my assistant would remind me of a networking event and I forgot to iron a dress—I could call The Kid, describe the dress, and ask him to iron it for me. He had my dress laid out, some shoes he thought would go with it, would zip the dress up for me, and have a plate of food ready on the counter. While this was rare in occurrence, the fact that my son was learning to think and survive on his own spoke volumes to one of my favorite Gandhi quotes: Be the change you want to see in the world.

I asked Kordelle one evening, "What does being black mean to you? How do you view your blackness?" Just out of curiosity. Saw a meme on Instagram earlier that day that piqued my interest, and as a young black man, I was curious of what his thoughts were. My mini skateboarded better than some white kids, was addicted to Japanese anime, was in love with sushi and Jamaican curry chicken, and had been begging me for red eye contacts. I cared about how society chose to categorize my eclectic introvert through *their* actions, not his. And if the label was applicable, why not discuss it? He said, "…it means being powerful and not bland." I thought that was a pretty unique answer.

I get annoyed by stuff. We all do. But I don't have the time or the patience to seriously try to set the whole world straight and save it. Matter of fact, that was already done and the world killed him, so then there's that. Maybe the answer to correcting the problem of our tainted children and misguided adults lies not solely in fixing our youth, but switching to loving our women that cultivate the youth; reminding or maybe principally showing women the power that they command.

Women are the sandwich in society plugging the holes in our broken men as well as our future kings; so much rests on the shoulders of our queens. What if we went back to loving them right? Respecting them? Addressing them like royalty? Women, what if we went back to respecting ourselves? The power that we would take back and then be able to successfully redistribute amongst our nation is monumental. The strength of a womb to transcend life from a world we can't see to a world we can has supremacy and clout that is given away for free far too frequently. Until our women wake back up, the change that I can single-handedly accomplish is to improve the inequalities of today by addressing pinpointed ideologies within my own young king.

#LUNCHBOXCHRONICLES

Capítulo Ocho

#Reflect

{Pausa... mira cuán lejos que has llegado}

Upon finishing undergrad, I had been in school for so long, taken so many random classes and changed my major so much that some classes wound up overlapping, and I qualified for two degrees. One was in Kinesiology, the other was in Abnormal Psychology. While I am unable to utilize this degree as a formal occupational practice until I attend grad school and complete clinical studies, I still have a vast basic foundation of psych principles. There was one that kind of evaded me, but I referred to its premise all the time. It was bothering me so heavy that I reached out to a psych-major home girl of mine, Diandra, at 6:34 a.m. one Saturday morning. I had questions about the premise of relativity that is displayed in a lot of movies such as *Karate Kid* (with Daniel-son), *Slum Dog Millionaire, Karate Kid* the remake (with Jaiden Smith) to name a few, where the connections between the subconscious mind spoke directly to the conscious mind.

In the first *Karate Kid*, Mr. Miyagi had Daniel- son painting the fence, sanding the floors, and waxing ON/waxing OFF each day he came to training. This wound up unconsciously transcending to other aspects of his life and he was able to superbly execute karate techniques in the final tournament in lieu of. In *Slum Dog Millionaire* because of all that Jamal had gone through in life, he was able to successfully answer the questions based on his indirect subconscious experiences. In the *Karate Kid* remake, modern Mr. Miyagi had Jaiden Smith learning to respect his mom and his things every time he came to learn karate. Jaiden's character repeated every day picking up his jacket, hanging up his jacket, taking off his jacket, throwing down his jacket. This cycle went on until Jaiden spazzed out on his sensei claiming, "You probably don't even know Karate!" Unbeknownst to him, the true karate moves that he wound up acquiring had already been disclosed to him while practicing respect for his mom and his clothes by picking them up off the floor and hanging them up.

When my friend Diandra called me back at a much more decent hour, she explained in further detail that Freud had started the studies of conscious relativity but passed away before he finished. Over the years, no one picked it back up. While she knew what I was referring to, there was no true real name for it. Being the type-A kind of person that I am, if something doesn't exist, I create it. Thus, by the conclusion of that call I had coined and claimed to name the psychological phenomena "Unconscious Relativity."

That term is what happens over life. We learn building block concepts in the confines of a safe, loving environment, practice and perfect them, and then go out into the world as able bodied self-sufficient adults. But what happens when those building blocks aren't introduced early enough? Or not at all.

When we have the opportunity to practice something, we get better at it over time. I am great at tying my shoes because I've had sooooooo many years to practice tying my shoes. I read aloud eloquently because

I've had years to practice reading aloud in the safe confines of a loving environment surrounded by adults to gently correct my mistakes to make me better.

Key examples of when that wasn't done on grand extreme scales are visible with the likes of society mocking Floyd Mayweather's inaudible reading skills a few years back and Fantasia's inability to read altogether. Oh but of course we presume that by the time people reach a certain age, as grown-ups, they are expected to be able to read, correct? Why is that? Because these are traits and activities we spend our whole lives perfecting. We've had decades to practice. Poor Fantasia couldn't read at all and Floyd struggled to read. The art of practicing said acts were missing over the years. Makes sense, right? Poor practice equals poor performance? That's a total no brainer when it comes to reading.

What about other life skills? What about when you wait 'til your child is fifteen to teach him or her how to wash clothes? How to cook? How to cut the grass? When you have a cook, a butler, a maid, and over coddling parent doing it all for them? What about when you wait 'til they are seventeen to teach them the importance of money? Or budgeting? Or financial independence and responsibility? Credit? Stocks? Or how to communicate properly and share vital info with loved ones like where they are going or when something is bothering them instead of holding it in? Or balancing a checkbook? What about when you wait 'til the yare eighteen to teach them how to fill out job or credit applications? Or how to ask for directions? I could go on for hours about the things I've noted that we wait way too long in life as the conglomerate masses to teach our children!

We are crippling our youth! Forcing them to figure it out super-fast at the last minute under our occasional watchful eye, or not at all forcing them to figure it out on their own, *if* they accomplish figuring it out at all. What if your child, now young adult, is a slow learner? Oh then they are just screwed huh? We toss them out in the world half learned to fend for themselves until they mess up somewhere along the way, make some grave life mistake, and have to come running back home for you to do the parenting you should have done back when they were ten. That learning curve doesn't go away. If a child requires ten years to perfect an action, and you wait 'til seventeen to show them, then of course they are going to still be figuratively stuck to your tit still nursing until about twenty-seven.

I see so many parents fussing about how their twenty-eight, nine, or thirty-year-old children can't function in full capacity. I'm always tempted to ask, "How do you expect them to?" To be honest, I blame parents. Our parents. My parents. Well not my parents directly… mine were pretty dope. They told me no. A lot. Planted the seeds, let God water them, and I grew. But oh trust I had some foundational holes as well.

But Generation X? I blame the deficiencies on our worldly cultivators. As I continued to rear my little one to survive in our new urban culture, it loudly dawned on me how much the masses cripple their offspring for one reason or another. I guess I get it: just because I understand the motives, it doesn't make the behavior acceptable, but trust. I get it. Growing up in an era when one had to go without for so long on so many different fronts, parents raising children in the late '80s early '90s who desired to provide their children with so much that they never had.

But this desire wound up enabling over-grown babies, removing the Unconscious Relativity, diminishing cognitive advancement for them to think, process, and function on their own two. Outside of any additional outliers of the '80s and '90s with the onset of drugs and rise in prostitution, I'm speaking on the basic desire that was executed in the average home to give kids better lives: that took away all the hard lessons that are needed to minimize American entitlement and sustain credible work ethic.

A bunch of grown ass babies. I stop and look at my peers and wonder, "How do you fix this?" I look at the world gone awry, the mental instability, and lacking psych health of young Americans. We weren't shown how to heal, just how to get by. We weren't shown how to endure, because the problems were always fixed. We weren't shown how to go without, because we received more of everything superficial and less core values. The over doing Christmas, the showering of birthday presents, the constant bailing out of problems, the gold stars for effort because the simply "tried". When have you EVER received a gold star for just waking up and living? We now live in a world of entitled grown up babies and we are passing these horrendous attributes to our kids.

I took a stand. That day in Baltimore when I could no longer afford certain luxuries that are expected and provided in the suburbs, my new city single mom entrepreneurial lifestyle said, "Nah Bruh... you goin' learn today."

I changed my work schedule for the first week, and made next to no money because massaging in a newly established practice from 9 a.m. to 2 p.m. wasn't really conducive to a new customer's schedule. But I made the sacrifice to get my mini on the right path of freedom.

I drove Kordelle to school every morning and rushed to work. I left work by 2 p.m., drove back to his school, was outside waiting for him by the time school let out, and navigated us successfully to the bus stop.

Coming from such a privileged background my damn self, I had NO idea how to ride the public bus. My ex-boyfriend from a few years prior was a bus driver in Baltimore City. I unblocked him from my phone list, humbled myself, and did a poor job of begging him to help me, a plea mixed with fear and pride.

It took him a few hours to process my request—I really struggle with asking for help. And through his light sighs and muffled giggles of how displaced I was, being as though he was born and raised in Baltimore, he helped me plot out a straight shot for my kiddo to get from school to home each day.

On the first day of school, the kid and I walked half a mile to the designated bus area and boarded the bus. I gave my mini over-the-top explicit instructions of how to conduct himself while on the bus: don't have your phone out on the bus if you don't have to. If you do, make sure you pay attention to who is around you and who may be watching you. When your stop comes, be the last one to get off of the bus. Look back at where you were sitting to make sure you didn't leave anything.

Before exiting the bus, I stopped and introduced myself to the bus driver for that route. Told him who I was, who my son was, and if there were any problems I had absolutely no problem sticking my size 9.5 shoe down the throat and out the ass of anyone who touched my baby. My son rolled his eyes but I could care less. The bus driver said that none of the kids were his responsibility or his problem. I retorted, "Yo, while I get that, I'm letting you know if something happens to my kid *I* would become his problem."

I asked when was the next time they changed routes. Annoyed, the driver told me their routes were switching in two weeks. I said, "Bet, Jesus loves you. I'll be back then." And sure enough, in two weeks from that day as well as every three months from then I would get on the bus and threaten every driver until I knew the whole rotation on a first name basis.

I rode the bus with the kid for the next three days. We would get off at the Walbrook Junction and then walk another half a mile from the stop to our house. Come the fourth day, my son told me that no other kid was on the bus with their mom and he didn't need me to ride with him anymore. Reluctantly, I agreed to meet him at the junction and we would walk home together. Come Friday, he told me he didn't need me anymore. THAT is all any parent truly wants from their kid… to raise them up to be self-sufficient enough to no longer need them, for them to be able to stand on their own two.

I gave a speech several years later about this same premise of Unconscious Relativity but instead of the Karate Kid, I used veal as an example.

I strongly despise veal to my core. Don't get me wrong, I'm a total meat eater, though these days due to the deregulation of the FDA, I have strongly been considering the pescatarian or vegetarian lifestyles. But veal has and will never be on my family's menu. When a young cow is born and designated to be herded for veal, it isn't allowed to stand. When a young cow stands, its muscles are strengthened. The meat becomes innervated with blood vessels and the meat becomes thick and tough. To prevent this from happening, the farmers break the cow's legs. Repeatedly. The young cow is bottle fed with nutrients and prevented from grazing. Its legs are broken for the rest of its short life and then it is put down for processing. I tried to put it nicely for anyone that still digs veal—do you.

But those actions are what we do to our youth every time we over coddle them. When we come to their rescue instead of allowing them to make their own decisions. Instead of being there to catch them if they fall, as over-loving parents, we prevent them from falling. But how do you ever get any stronger if you are never allowed to stand? What is life's worth if you never take any risks? The beauty in life is the balance it provides. God never intended for you to prevent them or even over protect them from living. When you over help, it turns into hindering.

We weren't put here to save our kids. We are only meant to love them. Let them make their mistakes, take their lumps, and learn to live life. Otherwise, we are generationally existing.

I can't control my son. As much as I would love to think I can, the only person I have full control over in this world is myself. I am simply put here as a guardian and a guidance. If he wants to make dumb decisions, great. If he wants to make great decisions, great. I remember I told him one day to never half-ass anything. If you are going to do anything in life, you commit to it. You go in all the way, no holds bar. If you are going to screw up, you commit to that screw up! Life is going to commit to the response you receive. And at the end of the day, when it is all said and done and you are standing in front of your maker, there will be no one to answer for the decisions you made in life but you. When you live, you live all the way. When you mess up, you mess up all the way. When you excel, you excel all the way. We don't half ass anything in this household. And rightly so, if I punish him 'I'mma reprimand him all the way. In life everything has a balance. Every action has an equal and opposite reaction.

Now, the kid thinks way more about whatever it is that he opts to do, because this is practice for the real performance. When he steps outside of my doors, he not only is a representation of me, but more importantly he is his own human. He is a young man living in a world governed by an entity that despises him. Being a Christian, I raise him with strong Christian values, and instill within him that the rest of the world does not think, act, or love as he does. But that should never deter him from maintaining his rock and values. However, to maintain, you must first know who you are. What do you like? What do you want? I laugh inside when we explore these principles and ideals, because I know so many adults that have no idea what they want.

When I give presentations and speeches across the country, as my businesses are now flourishing, I tell people that the two hardest things they will ever do in life is (1) answer and declare with audacity, *"Here's what I want!"* and (2) allow themselves to know that they deserve it.

Week one of riding the bus turned into week two. Turned into month one. Turned into month two. And I slowly started to see my little one grow into a man. I mean he would have eventually done so anyways, but with a much less commanding presence. Our travels became heavier.

His awareness of life surroundings changed as did our conversations. Kordelle asked me one day after seeing a marquee scroll across the bottom of the news channel, "When do you think things will get better mommy?" A black boy, Vonderrit Myers Jr. was gunned down not too far from where Mike Brown had been killed by an off-duty police officer who fired seventeen shots at him, as if the first three to five weren't enough. My theory of the heightened police brutality is a mixture of psychological compensation and authority extension.

I remember I briefly dated a Special Police Officer (SPO) a few years back. I was headed to drop off some food for him on my lunch break and mid commute, he canceled our meeting and said that they had some action on the property and he had to go. I wound up visiting with him the next day on site and the employed officers were all still talking about the take down.

The officers were hyped— glorified by how aggressive they were with the trespasser; they could finally put to use the take down techniques they had learned in training years ago. By the comments and slurs they recanted having hurled at the trespasser, you would've thought someone had invaded the White House lawn. Nope. They were assigned to some rink-a-dink, basic, no-big-deal, forgotten about government building tucked in Chevy Chase, Maryland. The training that they received mirrored that of soldiers; it was a mixture between basic police officers, soldiers, and hallway monitors all wrapped into one. And then they were stowed at a ridiculous building's babysitting job with all of this training and pent up aggression.

#Reflect

From the looks of it, I stereotypically and [admittingly] a bit judg-mentally presumed a lot of these guys were ignored throughout most of high school, maybe even a good portion of their lives. They wanted to be somebody. They wanted to be respected; revered. Tapping their knight sticks as they walked the empty halls of this uninhibited, barely-frequented building. The first opportunity that some silly immature kid wandered somewhere they didn't belong and these overly-aggressive anger implo-sive men with something to prove pounced. Now add some racism to this mix and you have a recipe for a national disaster, in the guise of security. Our people have been free for 150 plus years but are still mentally in bondage. Rounding out this theory, when you place weapons in the hands of mentally unstable, broken, unloved people, the power overtakes them. But unless we stop and address the root of our issues instead of attacking the symptoms, our children will continue to be gunned down like rabid dogs with hemorrhaging wounds and our responses like cute cartoon Band-Aids on the surface of the American flag. "Kordelle I think this won't start to improve until the people who are not affected start to care as much, if not more, than the people who are."

The SPO and I were short lived; when I noticed our issues in com-munication and unequally-yoked core values diminishing our connection, I lovingly pointed them out to him. He was unable to process my trepida-tions, stating that there was no disconnect and I was trippin'. I shook my head at him and said, "You are no different than entitled white folk in this country. While we scream our problems into the night as our children bleed out onto the streets, they can't help but lift their chins with pride incapable to see the evils below the crux of their turned-up noses. We speak in pain—they remain positioned like 'nah we good.' Smh, take care brother." He looked so confused as I walked off. Some people really can't smell when their shit stinks. I thank God for an open nose.

Kordelle and I watched the *Hidden Colors* series and used the exposures to discuss the confederate flags we saw on the side of the highway as we traveled through West Virginia. I no longer believe in shielding him from a world through which he is expected to navigate. No sir, take off your rose-colored glasses and see with crisp vision of our 'melanated reality.

I gave him financial books that I had laying around from my undergrad classes and required him to write book reports on them each week; he just had so much time on his hands and the child's aged appropriate books weren't challenging enough anymore. While I do note the finance books were a little much, children, just like any other entity on this planet, attempt to rise to the occasion of the expectations placed upon them. It may not be done gracefully or even successfully, but the attempts may cause one thing necessary for survival: growth.

We watch the news as child after child is persecuted, gunned down, guilty without a trial by the same enforcement charged to protect them. When has allowing one entity to be the judge and the jury ever been a good idea? Wrongful acts don't equate to execution: (pause) so because they thought he was guilty, the officer pulled the trigger... and we let the department walk?

The insatiable murders throughout the country of course sparked more conversations each evening over lunch box unpacking and news watching that compelled me to instruct Kordelle on how to conduct himself in the presence of an officer. My instructions killed me to deliver as they went against everything I have ever believed. I bow down to no one but God. I conform to nothing of this world unless it is of my choosing or God's command. Maybe I can twist this to sit right with me in God commanding me to educate Kordelle on officer conduct. But as I spent time taping his lunch box back together, because it was his favorite one and he didn't want to replace it, I told Kordelle that he didn't just need to pay attention to his surroundings in regards to someone that may want his shoes or his phone, but possible drug dealers that may want to recruit him to distribute drugs. He had a world of an audience each time he stepped out of the house and reviewing *now* how he should respond would prevent him from thinking irrationally via adrenaline and fear in the moment. Besides his peers, there were d-boys, non-minorities, animals, and cops.

When it came to most of the audiences, I told him that he could readily remove himself from the situation as long as there was no looming presence of acute danger. Maybe run into a nearby store or building. But when it came to cops? Don't run. Don't move. Don't reach for anything. Stand and breathe. I pointed out that not all cops were bad. Just like not all preachers were good. Spend time in your daily commutes practicing how to read situations and people. Behavior and body language speak volumes on emittance as well as on the receiving end. I told him to diffuse the threat in love, as it is better to be obedient than to sacrifice. Dead kids can't explain anything anyways. Kordelle listened and then said, "Ok."

While I remind my little one <u>often</u> that I'm winging this whole parenting thing, I had an inkling idea of how it was *supposed* to go; but that nurturing never included these convos or their dire answers. I was winging all of this too. In faith and fear. Kordelle asked who and how to trust. My answer to him is the same that I was given years ago after my first heartbreak: trust no man. The only person you should trust is God. Look for the God in everyone, if you don't see the Holy Spirit, don't let your guard down. Those are the same convos I was beginning to teach to the adults in my [massage] ministry, but the convos' originated from he and I.

I armor Kordelle with the word of God. Societally, we harp over the worldly battles that transpire amongst us, but through our disconnections with our Heavenly Father, we are unable to see the spiritual war raging around us. And just because we choose not to acknowledge this war doesn't mean it exists any less. One of the greatest tricks the devil ever executed was convincing the world that he doesn't exist. In continuing to learn my ever-changing child, he opened up to me that he struggles to fully understand the bible in attribution of how it's worded.

Bet. Scooped up a children's bible specifically broken down for boys. It's the coolest little thing! We go through it together each night and I'm like, "Yasssss God this breakdown is bomb!"

I never really spanked him again. Mainly because I am a product of the environment and while I know "spare the rod and spoil the child" being a young parent, I am also a realist. I am not so far removed from spankings to know that they absolutely do not deter bad behavior. If a child, or any person for that matter, wants to do something, no amount of physical punishment is going to stop that, because people are people. I found something that he strongly disliked and exploited it.

My son is a bookworm. As I'm typing this, he is sitting to the right of me at the dinner table reading something Zelda related right now. He loves science, experiments, and tinkering around with stuff to see how it works. But sports and physical activities are his nemesis. When my son gets out of line, which is rare (I think my over-the-top antics and outlandish bouts of crazy when he was younger left a lasting impression) he has exorbitant exercises to do.

In my own personal growth within business, studying the psychological mind-fuckings of how to motivate people to spend money, I learned that parenting and business were very very similar. Find what motivates people. Find their triggers. And stimulate them both. Figuring out what people don't like can be just as helpful as focusing on what they do. Knowing your target audiences pressure and pulse points can go a long way.

In alignment with most of humanity, we live in accordance to outdated regulations. As a society, we have outgrown the rules that govern us; they no longer apply to modern day civility. Our school systems fail our children and lag in sufficiently providing the necessary tutelage for communal success, as has corporate America—which adds to why I have been fired from every single job I have ever acquired.

I recently attended my baby brother's college graduation at Rochester Institute of Technology in upstate New York where allllllllllll of the super smart super nerdy engineers were excelling to their next chapter in life. One of the engineering disciplines was "Industrial Engineering." When I googled what that was I immediately knew that's what I should have gone to school for!

I had spent most of my time at different offices unwarrantedly telling them what was wrong with their establishments. In case no one ever told you, and you do the same thing: folk don't like that too much. When you go around pointing out problems in their company, AKA their baby—essentially calling their baby a bald-headed step child on the low, with all of their issues and problems, YOU become the problem. Folk don't like problems, just as much as they don't like change. Unless they request your advice, companies usually get rid of their occupational problems before they change their regulatory ones.

My mouth and strong disdain for authority landed me unemployed every time. So here I was, this blossoming small business owner by choice and by chance frolicking along through life trying to see the world; live in it and love it but not get sucked into to it. Raise a conscious black boy in a country that hates him. And serve God the best ways I knew how.

It ain't easy. I guess if it were, everyone would do it. But in my venting over the years, I've been able to touch a few people, inspire a few others, and encourage many just by staying true to my journey. My now ex-boyfriend (this book took some years to birth and people outgrow one another… no love lost just bad timing) used to be bothered by how much I would share online. But my walk, my massage business, my life IS my ministry. Along the way, you never know who your strength and testimony may help and touch. I believe in being a blessing, thus allowing others to be the same.

In believing that our sole purpose on this earth is to please and glorify God, all things we do are to exalt Him—why not share the moments? The good, the irritating, and everything in between. While heavily focused on my dreams and goals, life is what's happening in the meantime whether we want it to or not. With modesty, humility, and moderation, because the absolute best parts of my life are only explored by the people I experienced them with. I open my heart to others in hopes that my stories can help, heal, and inspire even just one young mother struggling for answers on how to raise her own conscious black boy in America.

I had a high school friend, Anita, reach out to me via Facebook messenger a few months back asking, "I just read your post…you leave my baby (referring to Kordelle) home alone?!"

"Uhhh… yea. I got stuff to do. He good."

We had boys the same age a few months apart. She opened up to me that she was terrified to leave her son alone by himself. She said that her son asked her too but she wasn't quite ready yet. I told her I would be too, but I didn't start because I wanted to, but because I had to. And he has been just fine ever since. Mentioned to her that her protecting him from life or what ever she thought she was doing was actually hindering his growth and enabling him to need her much longer than he needs to.

Leaving Kordelle alone charges him to learn responsibility, organization, timeliness, and punctuality to be at the bus stop on time. He has also learned communication skills: he has to text me when he gets to the bus stop, when he is on the bus, when he gets off of the bus, and when he gets home; he must communicate his wants and desires. I get packages dropped off at the house all of the time because I hate what I've dubbed "real people shopping." It's like Christmas all year round and he gets a kick out of opening my boxes.

He usually always asked, until one day, he didn't and accidentally opened a box that contained one of his *actual* Christmas presents. Now? I stress communication. But implementing such an important life skill throughout everything we do was initiated by him learning to stay home alone. It's never more than a few hours and I extend to him the same bout of courtesy in return with constant communication.

When I need something, I inform him. When I make it to a client safely, I text him and let him know (Kordelle worries more than an overprotective parent). When I would like something, I respect his time as a young adult and ask if he would be interested in doing XYZ with me, and give him the right to make a sound decision whether he does or not.

I take the time to explain certain life lessons that are integral parts of his upbringing like: why it is a bad idea to leave battery science experiments in my freezer unattended (insert deep eye roll HERE). Or, that while I understand he may be tired (insert another heavy eye roll), his mom is a baby bad ass; the expectations I place upon him are simply because I know he can handle them, and I expect his best. Not *thee* best, just his best.

I remind him of the life lesson we learned back in the cold Chicago airport about why we do not complain in our household (mainly because I don't want to hear it... HE USED TO REMIND ME ALL THE TIME)! OH MY, HOW QUICKLY WE FORGET: when you complain you have two options (1) change it, if you can't change it, (2) then you are to accept it. If you can't accept it, change it. If you can't change it, accept it. If you can't... you see where I'm going with this? But I explain why we don't complain [and then revisit the above options].

Or through loving communication, I actually elaborated on what talking back was. As he grew older, his smart mouth became more annoying and I would correct him with that same saying my parents hit me with, "Don't talk back to me!" Except to be honest, I never knew what that meant. I was encouraged to speak up and have an opinion, but not all the time? I was so lost. Once I noticed the same confusion in my little one, I broke down and explained what it truly meant. We haven't had much of a problem since. We... communicate.

The way I was raised? Tuuh... we got zero explanations! The answer was always, "Because I said so." In hindsight, I'm sure that's where my rebellious nature comes from. I just always needed to know stuff; when things make sense, it's like life giving me a big old comfort blanket snuggle.

Anita was blown away by the relationship my son and I had and the amount of trust, openness, and freedom I gave him. The kid has his own bike that he was too lazy to keep dragging in and out of the back-door cellar—I personally think it's because he's scared of the bugs in the cellar. But he asked me if he could leave the bike outside. I told him sure, but if it gets stolen, I'm not replacing it.

The next day on the way home, the kid asked me if he could ride his bike down the street. I told him go for it. Just look for cars and don't get snatched up—one of my typical responses. When I got home, he had three flowers laid out on the counter for me, a piece of my favorite candy, and a sparkling water I was currently addicted to.

Needless to say, I was super surprised and asked where he got all of this from. He told me, "I picked the flowers on the way up, and grabbed the candy and water when I rode my bike back down to the Rite Aid in the Junction. I walked through it earlier today when I got off the bus to see if they had any bike locks; they did. Rode my bike there and back to buy it, got you some stuff, and I have my bike locked around a support post out back." I asked him where he got the money from. He said he counted out coins from his piggy bank to cover the cost of the items plus tax.

He had his feet propped up on my Victorian couch playing a video game with the television blasting. I smiled. For the first time in a while, I was at a total loss for words. My only responses were (1) thank you love-bug, (2) in the future, make sure you continue to tell me the moves you make, and (3) get 'yo busted feet off my furniture!

The kid travels with me to most of my larger events. He recently took a liking to fly fishing and the best way to get better at it was to practice the back and forth technique. The kid took that damn fishing rod EVERYWHERE, including to one of my super important potential government contracts in DC. He was fly fishing in their historic antique 200-year-old rose bush with no pond, no fish, no water. Just him and some bushes. The director walked up to me and announced herself as I was peering out of the window at my mini. I introduced myself and said, "Sorry, was just checking on my little one." She responded, "Oh I figured that was your kid fishing with no fish. Especially once I saw your quirky attire and super cool tattoos. I totally knew he was yours. And we're happy to have you both; why don't we have a seat in my office."

That day his school was closed and he begged to come with me instead of stay at home. I myself was in no mood to dress up in any fancy attire to impress people who probably were going to judge me anyways. I stayed in my bright pink sweat pants, crisscross knit sweater, and baseball cap all day long. I mentioned it to my son's first principal at the beginning of our journey and damn if I wasn't proving it true: when you're good, people can deny you. Fault you. Discredit you for how they perceive you based upon any aspect of your appearance. But when you're great? All they see is the direct return on their investment and they don't give a damn what you look like—the only color they see is green.

It is super cool to be able to take him with me onto college campuses, larger contracts, and business ventures that I created from thin air (with faith and fear), giving him firsthand insight on the freedom being an entrepreneur brings. Our evenings are a lot less eventful these days. Especially once I found out that the kid gets free lunch no matter how much money you make AND you don't have to prove your income. Way less lost lunch bags. While our conversations were originally sparked when I was unpacking his book bag, him turning on the TV, us discussing life occurrences, and while I fussed over some lunch box mishap, we still maintained the connection along the way.

Nowadays, my son beats me to the conversations asking, "So mom how was your day?"

#Reflect

Our story had become so well known within the DMV (DC, Maryland, Virginia area) on and off social media platforms, between my fussing and the sharing of our hashtag #LunchboxChronicles, when people would meet me, usually clients, they would totally have a new lunch box for my baby. I now have a cabinet full of brand new lunch boxes that get us through the school year.

One day recently, I looked at him and he had underarm hair [insert dramatic silent whine HERE]. I paused and asked sheepishly, "Kordelle… do you… do you have pubic hair?" He whined back, "Maaaaaaaaaaaaaaa!" I fussed with my eyes closed, "I don't care if you don't want to share your personal info with me. Answer my question anyways!" He told me he did. Sigh. With a tinge of seriousness in my voice, I continued to fuss, "Stop it. Stop it right now! Stop growing up. I'm not ready! I demand you to cut it out!" He giggled and reached up like he always did when he was super young, gave me a kiss, and told me everything would be alright, "I'll always be your baby."

Leaving the University of Maryland football stadium after the players' practice, I gripped the wheel to stop from crying, accepting the reality that The Kid wasn't really a kid anymore. I mean, he was… but he wouldn't be forever. I hate when reality kicks my butt and I'm forced to grow out of seasons. I was still enjoying the current season in my life. I was not—am not—ready to move on. But reality is that life goes on. We change, we mature; we learn, experience, we develop. Who am I to challenge the system of life?

We still travel at a moment's notice. Currently, at age 10, he is much more aware of his surroundings. Now, he points out things I don't even notice and lightly makes fun of me when I miss them. We still have frequent talks about racism and prejudice, living in real life *Revelations*, we have no other choice but to talk about it. Since finishing grad school, being fired, and becoming my own mini mogul, the kid and I spend way more time together cooking and decorating the new house. He is still in love with Pringles.

It seems so surreal because I remember holding him for the first time, kissing him for the first time, looking into his dilated eyes for the first time as we rode home from the hospital terrified to death of what I was going to do with such a precious angel. I did the only thing I could—love him. Sigh… the kid is growing up before my eyes, and you know what? So am I.

PS - we still never had that sex talk.

For the road:

Jan 29, 2017 - Baltimore, MD
(Slight)#LunchboxChronicles

Mom: (packing lunch for tomorrow's field trip) Aye kid go to bed
Kid: ok. OH! I have an experiment in this container with salt, water, vinegar, and a battery. Don't open it. I'm charting its reaction time.
Mom: reacti...wait...wtf is gunna happen? And where did you get this battery from?!
Kid: The smoke detector. But its ok because it was beeping and old anyways. Oh, and there's gears on the table. Don't touch those either.
Mom: Wait wait wtf what gears where did you get gears from? Hol-up its my damn house i'll touch whatever i want... why cant i touch the gears?
Kid: (kisses me on the cheek while stealing baby carrots) Because they're electrically charged with negative ions; I want to see if the house's positive charge will effect them BUT they can be harmful to the touch...
Mom: (insert blank space here)
Mom again: (insert extra long blank stare here)
Mom still: How tf did you charge them Dexter?
Kid: That'll take too long to explain you told me go to bed right? (Walking up the stairs) and who is Dexter? Nvm love you mommy
I have... so SO many questions. Like... How tf did he get the smoke detector battery?! Wait...WHO TF PUTTING A NEW ONE IN I CANT REACH THAT!

#Reflect

March 20, 2017

Mom: Kid im throwing this lunchbox away. Its a hotmess. Besides, Mrs. Tarsha bought you a new one... wait...I thought i told you to collect all of the trash in the house kid? The trash can is still full. (Swerves into another room and does a basura check) and this one too! Kid?????!

Kid: Mom... trash is subjective

Mom: ...TF?!

Kid: One man's trash is another man's treasure

Mom: (silent long blink)

Kid: I didn't collect it because it's treasure mom

Mom: Kordelle... (long pause) i've already claimed you on my taxes for the year and it was approved. Don't make me make you come up missing. Collect this got damn trash 'fo you get tossed out with it... treasure my arse ARE YOU EFFIN SERIOUS?! You are NOT a pirate!

...smh tuuh treasure

ABOUT THE AUTHOR

Tai Hall

Serving as a strong public speaker, this millennial activist is an accomplished multi-business owner who courageously started her entrepreneurial journey after surviving several life setbacks including homelessness, dropping out of college, and being challenged to raise a young son in Baltimore City, a stark contrast to the Prince George's County Maryland suburbs they had uprooted from.

Dedicating her life to improving the quality of lives of others, Tai became an International Massage Therapist and a multiple business owner of Perfect Taiming Enterprises, LLC. She is well-versed on healing the body, cleansing the psyche, and mending the spirit. Tai holds a Bachelor's of Science degree in Neuromolecular Biomechanics, a Bachelor's in Abnormal Psychology, and a Master's degree in Healthcare from the University of Maryland College Park.

Today, Tai speaks to audiences across the world on entrepreneurship, healthcare, massage therapy, and everything in between.

Did you enjoy #LunchBoxChronicles?

Leave a review on Amazon.com and visit the #LunchBoxChronicles shop at TheLunchBoxChronicles.com.

www.ingramcontent.com/pod-product-compliance
Lightning Source LLC
Chambersburg PA
CBHW052007090426
42741CB00008B/1586